Information Technology Law in Montenegro

Information Technology Law in Montenegro

Andreja Mihailovic
Patricia Živković
Ivan Radević
Neli Rašović

This book was originally published as a monograph in the International Encyclopaedia of Laws/Privacy and Technology Law.

Founding Editor: Roger Blanpain
General Editor: Frank Hendrickx
Volume Editors: Jos Dumortier, Pieter Gryffroy, Ruben Roex & Yung Shin Van Der Sype

Wolters Kluwer

Published by:
Kluwer Law International B.V.
PO Box 316
2400 AH Alphen aan den Rijn
The Netherlands
E-mail: lrs-sales@wolterskluwer.com
Website: www.wolterskluwer.com/en/solutions/kluwerlawinternational

Sold and distributed by:
Wolters Kluwer Legal & Regulatory U.S.
920 Links Avenue
Landisville, PA 17538
United States of America
E-mail: customer.service@wolterskluwer.com

ISBN 978-94-035-3977-5

e-Book: ISBN 978-94-035-3987-4
web-PDF: ISBN 978-94-035-3997-3

The Authors

Andreja Mihailovic, PhD, is a lecturer, researcher, and consultant in the fields of business and criminal law, with a particular interest in cybersecurity, cybercrime, digital investigation, electronic evidence, cyber diplomacy, and innovation and technology policies. She is employed as a teaching associate for the criminal law group of subjects at the Faculty of Law of the University of Montenegro and engaged as a guest lecturer on the "Computer Crime" module at the University College Cork (UCC) in Ireland. She is involved in the development of the multidisciplinary information security study programs as well as various cyber-oriented initiatives addressing students' and the ICT market's contemporary needs. As a holder of a British Scholarship Trust scholarship, she was a PhD researcher at the University of Birmingham (UK) in 2017, where she gained advanced training in cybersecurity and digitalization (including: the Institute for Sociological and European Research (ISES, Hungary), the University of Tartu (Estonia), the Southeast European Dialogue on Internet Governance (SEEDIG, Moldova), the summer e-government academy of the Swedish Institute at the University of Linköping (SEGRID, Sweden), the Marie Curie Alumni Association "From Research to Innovation") and the summer school "EU and Legal Reform" (CCSDD, University of Bologna) and others. She has published a significant number of papers in prestigious domestic and international journals in the fields of commercial and criminal law, with a focus on digitization and cyber security. She participated in several projects aimed at improving corporate social responsibility, policy reforms, and cybersecurity education, and she was the project coordinator of the national team established by the Government and the University of Montenegro for the application for the location of the "Western Balkans Cyber Capacity Center (WB3C)," the project of the French Ministry of Foreign Affairs in collaboration with the Government of Slovenia, with the goal of creating a regional structure to strengthen cyber resilience and develop cyber capacities in the WB's economies and administrations. In 2022, she was selected as an expert in the field of digitization for the verification of knowledge, abilities, competences, and skills for work in state bodies by the Human Resources Administration of Montenegro, where she is also a trainer for training programs in the field of cyber security, Member of the European Law Institute (ELI) and the Executive Academic Board of the European Security and Defense College (ESDC).

The Authors

Patricia Živković, PhD, is a highly accomplished researcher in the fields of international commercial law and regulation of AI systems and biometric data, with her work focused on addressing legal issues in international dispute resolution, including commercial arbitration, as well as exploring the challenges and opportunities presented by the rapid development of AI-based technologies, particularly in the collection and processing of biometric data. Patricia joined the School of Law at the University of Aberdeen in 2019, bringing with her a wealth of expertise in international arbitration. She previously worked as an arbitration lawyer in Croatia, and she has actively promoted the use of alternative dispute resolution mechanisms as a co-founder of the Young Croatian Arbitration Practitioners, which is an association for younger members of the arbitration community in Croatia. In addition, she has extensive experience coaching students for the Willem C. Vis International Commercial Arbitration Moot Court and has served as an associate editor of the Kluwer Arbitration Blog. She also has in-house experience in the IT industry, having previously held the position of Head of Legal Department. Prior to joining the University of Aberdeen, Patricia held a position as an assistant professor at the International University of Sarajevo, where she coordinated and taught civil law courses. She received her undergraduate degree in 2011 from the Faculty of Law at the University of Zagreb and went on to earn an LLM degree in International Business Law in 2012, followed by an SJD (PhD) degree in 2016 from the Central European University in Budapest/New York. Her doctoral thesis, which examined the determination, payment, and allocation of costs in international commercial arbitration, was awarded the highest grade (summa cum laude). She is currently serving as the Associate Director of the Centre for Private International Law and is a member of the Centre for Commercial Law.

Ivan Radević, PhD, is a professor in the Department of Management and Organization at the University of Montenegro, Faculty of Economics in Podgorica. He is engaged in the following courses: Fundamentals of Management, Human Resource Management and Change Management. Also, since 2019, Ivan has been engaged at the Faculty of Electrical Engineering, University of Montenegro, in the course of Management in ICT. Before that, Ivan was a manager of the Faculty of Administrative and European Studies in Podgorica and an associate at the Department of Economics (2010–2015). Ivan is engaged as a lecturer in the Administration of Human Resources of Montenegro, as well as in the School of Rhetoric in Podgorica. He is a licensed state examiner in the field of informatics and a certified ECDL lecturer and examiner. For more than twenty-five years, Ivan has been active in his family's business—the printing house "Grafo Press" in Podgorica. He is one of the founders of the Sports and Recreational Association "Ekomen." Ivan obtained a master's degree in economics and in public administration legal studies. He defended his doctoral thesis in the field of management and organization—*Knowledge Management and Organizational*

Design as Quality Factors of Health Organizations' Services. He has published three books: "*Digital Economy and Marketing Management*," "*Rhetoric in the Function of Leadership*" and "*Knowledge Management and Organization: Healthcare Quality in Montenegro*" as well as many scientific papers. Ivan attended many educational programs and participated in a number of seminars and conferences on different topics in the field of economics in the country and abroad. He participated in the development of many projects and studies that are being implemented by the Government of Montenegro, Faculty of Economics in Podgorica and Faculty of Administrative and European Studies or were carried out in the past. Ivan is a member of the global professional association of scientists in the field of management and organization *Academy of Management* and of *Mensa of Montenegro*. For more details about the author, visit: www.ivan.me.

Neli Rašović, MSc, is the Representative of Montenegro at the Migration, Asylum, Refugees Regional Initiative (MARRI) Regional Centre (RC) in Skopje, seconded by the Government of Montenegro. Her main tasks are related to providing support to strengthen border management cooperation among the Western Balkans authorities. Prior to being seconded to the MARRI RC, her decade-long work experience was acquired within the Ministry of the Interior of Montenegro, where she served as an Advisor for International Cooperation, managing and coordinating a broad range of bilateral and multilateral activities. She has been involved in the EU Negotiation Process as Coordinator of the Institution for Chapter 23—Judiciary and Fundamental Rights. Continuously working on her personal and professional development, she has attended numerous programs and trainings in the country, as well as at eminent institutions across Europe and Asia (Sciences Po, College of Europe, Council of Europe, International Management Institute New Delhi, etc.). Her expertise and research interests cover several domains, including regional and international relations, migration, public administration reform, global and cyber security, and youth and female empowerment. Neli is a Chevening alumna and holds a Master's degree in International Relations from the University of Exeter, United Kingdom. She earned her Bachelor's degree in Economics from the Faculty of Economics, University of Montenegro. Neli speaks Montenegrin, Albanian, English, Italian, and some Spanish.

The Authors

Preliminary note for EU Member State monographies: Please do not explain the provisions of European and international legal instruments since these are dealt with in the EU monography. Simply refer to these provisions where relevant and focus on the specificity of the national legal framework.

Table of Contents

List of Abbreviations

AECPS	Agency for Electronic Communications and Postal Services
AEM	Agency for Electronic Media of Montenegro
AMS	Audiovisual and Media Services
CCDCE	Cooperative Cyber Defense Centre of Excellence
CEFTA	Central European Free Trade Agreement
CI	Critical Infrastructure
CIRT	Computer Incident Response Team
CSA	Cyber Security Agency
DPCI	Directorate for the Protection of Classified Information
ECL	Electronic Commerce Law
EU	European Union
GSM	Global System for Mobile Communication
HIF	Health Insurance Fund
ICT	Information and Communication Technologies
ITU	International Telecommunication Union
LAF	Law on Administrative Fees
LAP	Law on Administrative Procedure
LCEDUG	Law on Control of Export of Dual-Use Goods
LCI	Law on Classified Information
LCP	Law on Consumer Protection
LEC	Law on Electronic Communications
LED	Law on Electronic Documents
LEG	Law on Electronic Government
LEIES	Law on Electronic Identification and Electronic Signature
LFAI	Law on Free Access to Information
LHP	Law on Health Protection
LIMS	Laboratory Information Management System
LIS	Law on Information Security
LPDP	Law on Personal Data Protection
LTE	Long Term Evolution

List of Abbreviations

MDAF	Ministry of Defense and the Armed Forces
MPA	Ministry of Public Administration
NATO	North Atlantic Treaty Organization
NIS	National Intelligence Service
NSA	National Security Agency
NSO	National Statistical Office
OCCCD	Organized Crime and Corruption Control Department
OSCE	Organization for Security and Cooperation in Europe
PA	Public Administration
PIL	Private International Law
SCIS	Social Care Information System
UN	United Nations
WTO	World Trade Organization

General Introduction

Chapter 1. General Background of the Country

1. Montenegro is a country on the Balkan Peninsula in Southeast Europe with a total area of around 13,812 square kilometers (5,333 square miles).[1] The country's southwest coast, which extends 293 kilometers (182 miles) along the Adriatic Sea, is particularly notable for its varied and picturesque topography, which includes terrain ranging from mountains to valleys with a beautiful landscape. It shares borders with Bosnia and Herzegovina (225 kilometers to the northwest), Serbia (203 kilometers to the northeast), Albania (172 kilometers to the southeast), Kosovo (80 kilometers to the east), and Croatia (14 kilometers to the southwest).[2]

2. Podgorica, the administrative capital, is the country's largest city and economic center, covering 13,812 square kilometers (10.4% of Montenegro's territory).[3] Cetinje, the old royal capital, is a cultural and historic landmark as well as the headquarters of multiple institutions of the country, notably the official residence of Montenegro's President.

3. Montenegro has a long, highly complex history that runs throughout the centuries. The contemporary territory of Montenegro has been populated since prehistoric times. The Illyrians, an ancient Indo-European group, were the area's first documented inhabitants.[4] The name Montenegro first appears in historical records in 1296, in the edicts of the Nemanjic-dynasty Serbian monarch Stefan Uros I Milutin.[5] The term "Montenegro" derives from the Slavic phrase "Crna Gora—Black mountain," which refers to the vast, impenetrable forests that dominated the old Montenegrin mountains. Throughout history, multiple countries and dynasties fluctuated in Montenegro. The Duklja Principality emerged as the dominant political entity in the region in the ninth century. Duklja evolved into the Kingdom of Zeta

1. Nations online, "Republic of Montenegro/Crna Gora—Country Profile," https://www.nationsonline.org/oneworld/montenegro.htm, accessed Jun. 11, 2022.
2. Encyclopedia Britannica, "Montenegro," https://www.britannica.com/place/Montenegro, accessed May 7, 2022.
3. Capital city Podgorica, https://podgorica.me/en, accessed May 21, 2022.
4. John Boardman, The prehistory of the Balkans and the Middle East and the Aegean world. Cambridge University Press, 1982.
5. European Commission, Eurydice, Montenegro: historical development, https://web.archive.org/web/20190628190256/https://eacea.ec.europa.eu/national-policies/eurydice/crna-gora/historical-development_me, accessed Jun. 12, 2022.

in the fourteenth century. Within the twelfth century, the ruling dynasty of the Serbian Empire, the Nemanjic Dynasty, temporarily acquired control of Zeta. Following the downfall of the Serbian Empire, Zeta recovered its independence and fell under the control of the ruling families of Balsic and Crnojevic. In the fifteenth century, the Ottoman Empire began its expansion into the Balkans, and Montenegro experienced frequent incursions but preserved its autonomy in the mountainous regions. In 1878, Montenegrin's independence from Turkey was formally declared at the Berlin Congress.[6]

4. A few municipalities were added to Montenegro's territory after the Berlin Congress, which accelerated the country's economic growth. Under the authority of notable monarchs, such as Peter I and Peter II, Montenegro fortified its institutions and modernized its government. Prince Nikola, observant of the significance of the legal system to the performance of society, initiated the adoption of the General Property Code, which was codified in 1888 by Valazar Bogisic.[7] With origins in Roman law, Montenegro's legal system belongs to the continental European legal tradition. The first Montenegrin Constitution (based on the principle of sovereignty) was enacted in 1905, followed by the first Criminal Code in 1906 and the Commercial Code in 1910.[8]

5. The political events that accompanied the First World War interrupted the country's autonomy, stability, and legal system development. In the 1918 state, the Kingdom of Serbs, Croats, and Slovenes (later named the Kingdom of Yugoslavia),[9] Montenegro kept a certain degree of autonomy within Yugoslavia, but its political standing altered throughout the course of time. In the context of the legal system, the previous private law was maintained through the provisions of the General Property Code but was not codified in all of its components. In the early 1990s, following the disintegration of Yugoslavia, Montenegro continued in a state union with Serbia, constituting the Federal Republic of Yugoslavia.

6. On June 3, 2006, Montenegro announced its independence from Serbia after a referendum that took place on May 21, 2006, in which 55.5% of Montenegrins opted in favor of independence.[10] Following its independence, Montenegro became the 192nd member of the United Nations (UN) and the Organization for Security and Cooperation in Europe (OSCE). In addition, Montenegro is a member of the Council of Europe, the Central European Free Trade Agreement (CEFTA), and the

---

6. Raspopović, R., "On the historical significance of the decisions of the congress in Berlin for Montenegro," Historical Records, 91(3/4), 16–19 (2018), https://istorijskizapisi.me/wp-content/uploads/2021/01/3.-Radoslav-Raspopovic-O-istorijski-znacaju-odluka-kongresa-u-Berlinu-za-Crnu-Goru.pdf, accessed Jul. 11, 2022.
7. Jelena Danilović (1998). Foreword to Valtazar Bogišić, General Property Code for Principality of Montenegro. Belgrade—Official Gazette, Podgorica—Unirex. p. 30.
8. Jokić, Lj. (2002). State legal history of Montenegro, Podgorica 2002, 110–112.
9. Kamusella, Tomasz (2009). The politics of language and nationalism in modern Central Europe. Palgrave Macmillan. pp. 228, 297.
10. The Republican Commission for the Implementation of the Referendum on the State Status of the Republic of Montenegro, https://web.archive.org/web/20060720151606/http://www.rrk.cg.yu/aktuelnosti/aktuelnosti.htm, accessed Jul. 12, 2022.

World Trade Organization (WTO), enabling the country to actively engage in international trade, take advantage of trade regulations, and gain access to foreign markets. Since December 2010, Montenegro has been a candidate for membership in the European Union (EU) and has generated significant progress in harmonizing its policies and legislation with EU standards.[11] Nevertheless, the Montenegrin accession process is quite challenging and requires additional improvements in different domains in order to comply with an extensive list of requirements. Montenegro joined the North Atlantic Treaty Organization (NATO) on June 5, 2017, as the 29th member, providing guarantees of security and enhancing its defensive capacity through association with other Member States.[12]

7. Montenegro's current Constitution was officially introduced on October 22, 2007,[13] replacing the Constitution from 1992. The Constitution outlines Montenegro as an independent civic, democratic, and sovereign state of social justice with a republican form of government. The preamble outlines the commitment of the citizens of Montenegro to live in a state in which the basic values are freedom, peace, tolerance, respect for human rights and liberties, multiculturalism, democracy, and the rule of law.[14]

8. It is interesting that Montenegro was the first constitutionally declared ecological state when the Montenegrin Parliament ratified the "Declaration on the Ecological State of Montenegro" on September 20, 1991, in Zabljak.[15] The provision on Montenegro as an ecological state was also incorporated into the current Montenegrin Constitution.

9. In accordance with the most recent official data published by the National Statistical Office (NSO), the country has 616,695 inhabitants.[16] According to the 2011 Census results, Montenegrins represent 44.98% of the population based on their citizenship affiliation, followed by Serbs (28.73%), Bosnians (8.65%), Albanians (4.9%), Muslims (3.31%), and Croats (0.98%). The Constitution establishes Montenegrin as the state's official language and equates the Cyrillic and Latin alphabets in legal standing. Serbian, Bosnian, Albanian, and Croatian are also recognized as languages in official usage.

10. The allocation of power in Montenegro is governed by the principles of balance and division between legislative, executive, and judicial authority. The Constitution, laws, and secondary legislation of Montenegro define precisely the

---

11. European Union External Action, The European Union and Montenegro, https://www.eeas.europa.eu/montenegro/european-union-and-montenegro_en?s=225, accessed Jan. 15, 2023.
12. NATO, https://www.nato.int/wearenato/montenegro.html, Jan. 15, 2023.
13. Montenegro's Constitution of 2007, https://www.constituteproject.org/constitution/Montenegro_2007.pdf, Mar. 3, 2023.
14. Article 1 of the Montenegro's Constitution.
15. Environmental Protection Agency of Montenegro, "Declaration on the Ecological State of Montenegro," https://epa.org.me/deklaracija-o-ekoloskoj-drzavi/, accessed Jul. 11, 2022.
16. MONSTAT, Statistical Office of Montenegro, "Population estimations—Data," http://www.monstat.org/eng/page.php?id=234&pageid=48, accessed Feb. 15, 2023.

composition of powers, capacities, supervision, and the process of decision-making. The president has been elected directly for a period of five years and represents Montenegro in the country and abroad.[17] The legislature's authority is exercised by the unicameral Parliament, which is composed of eighty-one members elected directly for a four-year term on an equitable basis by a universal and equal vote.[18] The Government of Montenegro is Montenegro's primary executive authority, led by the Prime Minister, Deputy Prime Ministers, and ministers elected by the Montenegrin Parliament.[19] The judicial branch has been established on the fundamental principles of autonomy and independence and rules in accordance with the Constitution, laws, and ratified international treaties.[20]

11. The Constitution stipulates the right to local self-government, which includes the right of citizens and local self-government bodies to govern and oversee certain public and other activities under their own responsibility and for the benefit of the residents of the area. The municipality is the main form of local self-government, but additional types of local self-governments are conceivable.[21]

17. Article 95 of the Montenegro's Constitution.
18. Article 83 of the Montenegro's Constitution.
19. Article 102 of the Montenegro's Constitution.
20. Article 118 of the Montenegro's Constitution.
21. Articles 113 and 114 of the Montenegro's Constitution.

Chapter 2. Telecommunications Infrastructure

12. The telecommunications infrastructure in Montenegro has expanded substantially in recent years, providing a wide range of services and enhancing connections throughout the entire country. An advanced and effective telecommunications infrastructure was successfully created in Montenegro in order to provide a wide range of communication channels, notably fixed and mobile phone services, internet access, and broadcasting. Based on forecasts, the dynamics of this expansion will continue to accelerate in the near future, mostly as a result of the high level of demand for IT services in the public, economic, educational, and health sectors. Due to these factors and the synergistic effects it has with other priority sectors, Information and Communication Technologies (ICT) has been identified as a horizontal priority industry in the national Smart Specialization Strategy, with the potential to stimulate substantial growth within all industries.[22]

13. Since the 1980s, when the sector began to privatize, the greatest number of expenditures on ICT infrastructure have been made by the private sector. The government's monopolistic telecommunications and broadcasting infrastructure structure has been substantially substituted by the increasingly open marketplace for fixed and mobile services. That initiated the demand for increased customer expectations for higher-quality services, flexibility, faster access rates, and a broader choice of internet and media services. The authorities have been employing several kinds of market measures involving: market demand stimulation (such as implementing eGovernment services); targeted public incentives for promoting private investment in remote areas, particularly through public-private partnerships; and public funding in broadband infrastructure for the distribution of government services and the establishment of resources for private operators. Private participation also contributes to the development of commercially sustainable, long-term programs in comparison to those that are continuously dependent on government assistance.[23]

14. As primary challenges related to accelerating the growth of telecommunication infrastructure, two strategic goals are pursued: (1) optimizing the abilities and potential for digital transformation; and (2) increasing the digital awareness of Montenegrin society and the digital competitiveness of the ICT sector. In regard to the Digital Transformation Strategy, the ICT Committee prepared a SWOT analysis of the ICT industry, providing an insightful conceptual framework and foundation for further advancement. The following benefits are identified:

- the appearance of international companies and outstanding research teams; Established higher education system;
- the presence of a competent workforce;

22. Ministry of Education of Montenegro, Smart Specialisation Strategy of Montenegro 2019–2024, https://www.gov.me/dokumenta/ea1d661e-922a-4d42-af8d-ae55bc53988e, May 7, 2022.
23. European Bank for Reconstruction and Development, "Investor Perceptions and the Broadband Sector: South Eastern Europe Region & Montenegro," Brussels: Cullen International, 2020, 13.

- attractive location and size of the country for pilot projects that leverage cutting-edge technologies;
- the environmental protection and variety of natural resources;
- optimal telecommunication facilities;
- effective legal and institutional framework.

15. The most significant weaknesses of the ICT sector are outlined as:

- insufficient "critical mass" in the academic community in the domain of technological advancement caused by dispersion and the lack of cooperation;
- inadequate transfer of knowledge and technologies from European knowledge centers with limited ties of research and development facilities with the business sector;
- the lack of funding as well as involvement of the public and private sectors in study and development initiatives that address the basic requirements of micro and small businesses.[24]

16. In accordance with current progress and the concept of Industry 4.0, ICT in Montenegro represent a major factor in optimizing the competitiveness of the entire national economy. The ICT sector's contribution to GDP is 4.1%, with an ongoing increasing trend, as reported in the most recent annual statistical analysis of the NSO of Montenegro. Based on the same analysis, the percentage of Internet penetration is quite high, with over 80% of households and 100% of companies connected to the Internet in 2022, while 85% of companies have a web presentation, which is 5% more than in 2018.[25] According to the data from the report of the Chamber of Commerce of Montenegro, the proportion of ICT in the overall economy in regard to the number of companies is 5%, the percentage of employees is 4%, the percentage of income is 5%, and the percentage of revenue is 4%, according to key indicators: companies, employees, income, and revenue.[26] The country's advancement in digital technologies is anticipated to be supported by continuing investments in broadband infrastructure, which will further improve the telecommunications environment.

17. Electronic communications at the national level fall into the category of infrastructural industries, and investments in telecommunications and information infrastructure are one of the main drivers of economic progress. Over the past decade, electronic communication service providers in Montenegro have invested more than EUR 650 million. Since 2016, which was the most successful year ever for investments, the upward trend of high-degree investments has been particularly evident. Based on official data, electronic communication operators in Montenegro invested EUR 68,789,048.31 in electronic communication network development in

---

24. Ministry of Public Administration of Montenegro, "Digital Society and Media, Montenegro Digital Transformation Strategy" 2022–2026, 75–76.
25. Monstat, Statistical Office of Montenegro, Statistical yearbook 2022, http://monstat.org/eng/novosti.php?id=3646, Mar. 15, 2023.
26. The Chamber of Commerce of Montenegro, https://komora.me/wp-content/uploads/2022/12/cg-privreda-2022.pdf, Mar. 3, 2023.

2022. These investments represent a 33.54% increase compared to the EUR 51,511,566.14 invested in 2021. This establishes a firm foundation for increasing the availability and quality of electronic communication services throughout Montenegro. Through these networks, users in Montenegro have access to all electronic communication services offered in advanced economies, consequently fulfilling their requirements. Major operators have migrated their networks to an "all-IP" environment, providing voice transmission, data transmission, and AVM content distribution over a unified IP network. According to public statements, operators in Montenegro's electronic communication sector intend to invest approximately EUR 65 million in 2023, EUR 44 million in 2024, and EUR 45 million in 2025. Continuous high investment in the electronic communication sector demonstrates the reliable and stable regulatory framework in Montenegro, which has led to equal conditions for all market participants.[27]

18. The growth of electronic communications is dependent on the availability of the necessary infrastructure to support the networks and related components that enable operators to offer electronic communication services. Through utilizing the electronic communication infrastructure of other operators and owners of communal and other equipment, operators without their own infrastructure are permitted to rapidly and economically install their electronic communication networks. The Law on Electronic Communications (LEC) has stipulated the obligation of shared use of electronic communication infrastructure for the purposes of rational use of space, environmental protection and public health, national security, spatial planning and protection of cultural heritage, construction and use of electronic communications networks, electronic communications infrastructure, and associated facilities. The operator shall perform its activity in a manner that enables the shared use of elements of electronic communications infrastructure and associated facilities in accordance with the available capacities.[28] Provided that such usage is technically possible and does not interfere with the use of such infrastructure and connected facilities, operators must agree to the shared use of electronic communications infrastructure and related facilities. The contract will specify the parties' mutual rights and duties for the shared use of the equipment and electronic communications infrastructure.[29]

19. Additionally, the Law on the Use of Physical Infrastructure for the Installation of Electronic High-Speed Communication Networks regulates the shared use

27. The Agency for Electronic Communications and Postal Services of Montenegro, "High Level of Investment in the Sector of Electronic Communications In Montenegro," https://www.ekip.me/latest-informations/announcement/visok-nivo-investicija-u-sektoru-elektronskih-komunikacija-u-crnoj-gori, Mar. 21, 2023.
28. Article 53 of the Law on Electronic Communications ("Official Gazette of Montenegro," Nos. 040/13 from Aug. 13, 2013, 056/13 from Dec. 6, 2013, 002/17 from Jan. 10, 2017, 049/19 from Aug. 23, 2019).
29. Article 54 of the Law on Electronic Communications.

and coordinated construction of physical infrastructure, such as ducts, poles, conduits, control rooms, cabinets, buildings or building entrances, and antenna installations.[30] By enabling the installation of multi-purpose infrastructure throughout the country, it significantly facilitated the development of high-speed electronic communication networks and the implementation of the new technologies in a cost-effective manner, especially given the high costs of construction work on the installation of networks. In this way, networks are deployed more rapidly, costs are reduced, and cultural heritage and space are protected as some of the most important national resources. An integrated and coordinated approach to the utilization of electronic communication infrastructure is a significant prerequisite for the efficient development of ICT in Montenegro.

20. The shared use of electronic communication infrastructure is continuously increasing, and it has contributed to improved coverage of broadband access networks in Montenegro. According to the data from the Agency for Electronic Communications and Postal Services (AECPS), currently, 85.12% of households have access to fixed broadband internet, and mobile broadband covers 97% of the population. Furthermore, internet connections with speeds exceeding 100 Mbps are available to 78.46% of households. The technologies used for providing fixed broadband access to households include: 71% FTTx (fiber-to-the-x), 69% VDSL (very high-bit-rate digital subscriber line), 49% HFC (hybrid fiber-coaxial), and 18% ADSL (asymmetric digital subscriber line). Currently, operators share the following:

- Telecommunication cable ducts span 710 kilometers, which is twice as much as in 2015.
- Space on 333 antenna towers, accounting for 55% of the total number of antenna towers in Montenegro.
- Space in 228 telecommunication facilities, representing 31% of the total number of telecommunication facilities in Montenegro.
- Street lighting poles in eight municipalities in Montenegro.[31]

21. With the use of GPON technology, fixed-line electronic communication providers in Montenegro have created access networks based on fiber optic cables that provide much faster internet access speeds and greater service quality for end customers. Every municipality in Montenegro has FTTH/B access networks available to end customers, and it is estimated that by the end of 2022, 71% of households had FTTx coverage, 69% had VDSL, 49% had HFC, 18% had ADSL, while around 15% of households lacked fixed broadband access. The transport networks of operators are implemented using state-of-the-art SDH equipment from renowned global

30. Article 3 of the Law on the Use of Physical Infrastructure for the Installation of Electronic High-Speed Communication Networks ("Official Gazette of Montenegro," No. 001/22 from Jan. 10, 2022).
31. The Agency for Electronic Communications and Postal Services of Montenegro, "Shared Use of Electronic Communications Infrastructure," https://www.ekip.me/latest-informations/announcement/zajednicko-koriscenje-elektronske-komunikacione-infrastrukture, Mar. 21, 2023.

equipment manufacturers (Siemens, ECI, Huawei). The maximum network capacity is 10 Gb/s (STM64) and is used for the transmission of SDH and EoS (Ethernet over SDH) traffic. The SDH backbone network is mostly implemented in a ring topology to ensure service protection. A smaller portion of the SDH backbone network has a linear topology in areas where a ring topology was not physically feasible. There are also local SDH rings and chains for the aggregation of SDH and Ethernet traffic at the local transport level. An infrastructure that permits fast IP traffic transmission across Montenegro is the MPLS transport network. All businesses may use basic IP communication services for establishing connections between remote areas and central locations using the MPLS network, and they also have the option to utilize the MPLS network to deploy additional services. These services are built upon cutting-edge technologies that enable automated system configuration, high security for end-to-end network transport, priority of business activities over the transport network, and sophisticated network monitoring and management capabilities. The MPLS network is also used as a transport network to provide consumers with broadband services, including IPTV and broadband internet access.[32]

22. In terms of population coverage by mobile network signals, Montenegro can be compared to the most developed nations in Europe in terms of public mobile electronic communication networks. Specifically, the overall population coverage by Global System for Mobile Communication (GSM) signals is approximately 99%, while the combined coverage of UMTS and Long Term Evolution (LTE) networks is approximately 98%, positioning Montenegro among the countries with the highest level of penetration. Mobile network signals reach nearly all populated areas, including urban and suburban regions, the majority of rural areas, significant traffic routes (including tunnels), and popular tourist destinations. Software predictions indicate that GSM coverage comprises approximately 84% of Montenegro's total territory, while UMTS and LTE coverage extends beyond 80%. Utilizing the mechanism of universal service, efforts are being made to enhance coverage in the remaining sparsely populated areas. With regard to Montenegro's challenging topography, the radio access component of mobile networks operated by all three providers is dependent on a substantial number of radio base stations, which are continuously growing. Crnogorski Telekom had 401 active base/repeater stations for external and tunnel coverage at the end of 2022, One Crna Gora had 438 stations, and Mtel had 373 stations. The radio access component of GSM/DCS1800 networks operated by all three providers operates in the 900 MHz frequency band and partially in the 1800 MHz band, with 392 radio base stations in the networks of Crnogorski Telekom, 422 in the networks of One Crna Gora, and 358 in the networks of Mtel. The UMTS access component operates in the 2 GHz and 900 MHz bands and includes a significant number of Node B stations (277 in Crnogorski Telekom's network, 426 in One Crna Gora's network, and 295 in Mtel's network by the end of 2022). The installations in the access components of GSM/DCS 1800 and UMTS networks are gradually declining, and the freed spectrum is being allocated to the placement of LTE and NR technologies. The access component of LTE/LTE-Advanced networks

32. Agency for Electronic Communications and Postal Service of Montenegro, "Work Report for the 2022 Year," Podgorica, 2023, 26.

operated by all three providers represented the most significant advancement in the evolution of mobile electronic communication networks. In 2022, Crnogorski Telekom had deployed LTE radio base stations at 377 locations in the 800 MHz, 1800 MHz, 2 GHz, and 2.6 GHz bands (the base coverage of Crnogorski Telekom's LTE network reaches approximately 97% of Montenegro's population, while coverage for data transmission services with a minimum throughput of 10 Mb/s is available to 96.8% of the population). In the access component of Crnogorski Telekom's LTE network, there were 198,175 active PRB (primary resource block) blocks at the end of 2022, an increase of over 30% from the end of 2021.[33]

23. In accordance with the Law on Digital Dissemination ("Official Gazette of Montenegro" No. 34/11), analog television signal broadcasting ended on June 17, 2015, in Montenegro. Since then, the focus has been exclusively on the development of digital terrestrial broadcasting, which utilizes terrestrial stations for digital television signal transmission.[34]

24. In terms of the deployment of 5G mobile networks, Montenegro completed the technical and legal framework in 2021, both in the frequencies previously allocated to mobile operators and in the latest-generation 5G bands.[35] At the end of 2021, the Government of Montenegro adopted the Roadmap for the introduction of 5G mobile communication networks in Montenegro, which specified concrete activities for the introduction of 5G technology and the commercial availability of 5G services in Montenegro by the end of 2022.[36]

25. From the beginning of 2022, the allocation of available radio frequencies from the 2 GHz and 2.6 GHz bands was finalized, allowing mobile operators to employ dynamic spectrum sharing (DSS) methods to use a portion of their current resources for the deployment of 5G technology. Crnogorski Telekom and One Crna Gora commercially stationed 5G networks based on DSS technology in March and July 2022, respectively. Radio frequencies from the 2 GHz band are the basis of Crnogorski Telekom's NR (DSS) network, whereas One Crna Gora makes use of frequencies from the 1800 MHz, 2 GHz, and 2.6 GHz bands. With the exception of five municipalities (Andrijevica, Petnjica, Pluzine, Savnik, and Tuzi), Crnogorski Telekom has installed around 80 NR (DSS) radio base stations by the end of March 2023, covering almost 75% of Montenegro's population and offering 5G services in all other municipalities. With 5G coverage accessible in Bar, Berane, Bijelo Polje, Cetinje, Niksic, Podgorica, and Tivat, One Crna Gora's network has over 30 active NR (DSS) radio base stations.

---

33. *Ibid.*, 27–29.
34. The Law on Digital Broadcasting ("Official Gazette of Montenegro" No. 34/11).
35. Institute for Research Development in the Field of Occupational Safety, Study on the Strategy of Introducing 5G Mobile Communication Networks in Montenegro, Podgorica, 2021.
36. The Government of Montenegro, "Strategy for the Development of 5G Mobile Communication Networks in Montenegro 2023–2027," https://www.gov.me/dokumenta/751e756a-c606-43f4-b9d6-778fbdc4b4b3, Apr. 22, 2023.

26. The allocation of 5G frequency bands, particularly in the 3.6 GHz band, creates conditions for the development of 5G networks capable of delivering data transmission speeds in the order of Gbps and later-stage services characteristic of 5G. Each licensee is required to provide network coverage to at least 98% of Montenegro's population by the end of 2026, enabling functional data transmission to users at speeds of 10 Mbps or higher and to at least 75% of the population at speeds of 30 Mbps or higher. By the end of 2030, speeds of 100 Mbps or higher must be achievable, and coverage should include at least five uncovered rural areas as well as continuous signal coverage along all highways and major roads in Montenegro. By the end of 2024, 5G networks will be available in every municipality in Montenegro, reaching at least 50% of the total population by 2026 and covering all populated areas, highways, and major roads by 2030. In the forthcoming period, mobile operators will need to construct electronic communication infrastructure and deploy equipment at various places, including a sizable number of completely new sites, in order to satisfy these needs. Additionally, the adoption of this technology by certain vertical industrial sectors and end users is a necessary condition for it to reach its full potential and be fully utilized in Montenegro.

Chapter 3. The Information and Communications Technology Market

27. The Montenegrin electronic communications market at the end of 2022, based on the AECPS, is represented below:

- The total number of fixed telephony subscribers in Montenegro is 190,000.
- The penetration rate in the mobile telephony market is 205.5%.
- 75.8% of the population is covered by 5G network signal.
- The total number of fixed broadband internet subscribers is 196,270.
- 46% of users have a fiber optic connection, while 55.64% of users have speeds of 100 Mb/s or higher, and nearly 71% have speeds exceeding 30 Mb/s.
- Fiber optic connectivity is available to 71% of households.
- Compared to the previous year, the total fixed internet traffic has increased by 47%, and the average monthly traffic per user has increased by 41%.
- The number of audio-video media service subscribers increased by 4.6% in 2022.
- Compared to the previous year, the total mobile internet traffic has increased by 41%, and the average monthly traffic per user has increased by 27.7%.[37]
- The level of user satisfaction with the quality of electronic communication services ranges between 78.5% and 84.0%, whereas satisfaction with prices ranges between 61.9% and 71.0%.[38]
- The Digital Economy and Society Index DESI index for Montenegro is 35.1, which is the highest among the Western Balkan countries but lower than the EU average.[39]

28. In the official Register of Electronic Communication Service Providers in Montenegro,[40] there are thirty-four operators authorized to provide the following activities:

- implementation of public fixed electronic communication networks and related services;
- establishment of public mobile electronic communication networks and provision of associated services;

37. Agency for Electronic Communications and Postal Services, "Overview of the electronic communications market in Montenegro," 2023, https://www.ekip.me/latest-informations/announcement/odrzana-prezentacija-pregled-trzista-elektronskih-komunikacija-u-privrednoj -komori-crne-gore, Mar. 29, 2023.
38. Chamber of Commerce of Montenegro, "Economy to better use the benefits of the 5g network," https://komora.me/poslovni-ambijent/privreda-da-bolje-iskoristi-benefite-5g-mreze, Mar. 29, 2023.
39. Montenegro business, "Montenegro is on top of the Western Balkan when it comes to Digital Economy and Society Index," https://montenegrobusiness.eu/montenegro-is-on-top-of-the-western-balkans-when-it-comes-to-digital-economy-and-society-index/, Mar. 29, 2023.
40. Agency for Electronic Communications and Postal Services, Register of Electronic Communication Service Providers in Montenegro, https://ekip.me/table/electronic-communications/ek-operators-register, Mar. 28, 2023.

- utilization of public fixed electronic communication networks using fixed wireless access (FWA) and provision of related services;
- providing a public voice over internet protocol (VoIP) service;
- offering public internet access services;
- providing public leased line services;
- implementation of public electronic communication networks for transmitting and broadcasting radio and other signals, along with the provision of public electronic communication services for signal transmission, broadcasting, leased lines, and multiplexing;
- deployment of public cable electronic communication networks and provision of public electronic communication services for distributing radio and television programs to end-users;
- providing public electronic communication services via their own functional network or system;
- implementation of public electronic communication networks based on broadband wireless access (BWA) and provision of related services;
- providing IP telephony, callback, and information center services;
- providing wireless internet access services in the 2.4 GHz and 5 GHz radio frequency bands;
- providing digital leased line services for national and international connections;
- offering dark fiber leasing services;
- providing services such as internet access, voice transmission over internet protocol (VoIP), video streaming, faxing, voice services, point-to-point Ethernet connections, and IP transit;
- providing access to and usage of electronic communication network elements and leasing electronic communication infrastructure;
- implementation of electronic communication networks based on the Terrestrial Trunked Radio (TETRA) standard, including voice and short text message transmission services via TETRA systems;
- providing public electronic communication services via satellite, including internet access and leased line services;
- providing public telephone booth services and voice transmission over internet protocol networks.[41]

29. Fixed telephony services in the territory of Montenegro are provided by four operators: Crnogorski Telekom, Mtel, Telemach and One Crna Gora. The number of fixed telephony service accounts at the end of 2022 was 190,595, representing a market penetration of 30.74%. In comparison to the previous year, the total number of fixed telephony service users increased by 0.57%.[42]

41. Agency for Electronic Communications and Postal Service of Montenegro, "Work Report for the 2022 Year," Podgorica, 2023 33–34.
42. *Ibid.*, 35.

30. Figure 1 represents the number of fixed telephony service accounts in Montenegro 2010–2022)[43] represents the total number of fixed telephony service accounts in Montenegro for the period from 2010 to 2022, along with the market penetration share.

Figure 1 The Number of Fixed Telephony Service Accounts in Montenegro 2010–2022

31. Regarding the quantity and structure of fixed telephony traffic in Montenegro in 2022, users of all four fixed operators achieved 70,546,872 minutes of outgoing traffic. Total outbound traffic from the Crnogorski Telekom network was 81.28%, outbound traffic from the Mtela network was 14.67%, and outbound traffic from the Telemach network was 3.45%, while the proportion of outbound traffic from the One Montenegro network was 0.60%. In Montenegro, natural persons own 85.67% of all fixed telephone lines, while legal entities own 14.33%.[44]

32. In the Montenegrin mobile telephone market, there are three service providers: One Crna Gora, Crnogorski Telekom, and Mtel. According to the most recent market penetration reports, the total number of mobile telephone service accounts in Montenegro at the end of 2022 was 1,274,031, representing a market penetration of 205.48% and an increase of 13.75% from the previous year.[45]

43. *Ibid.*
44. *Ibid.*, 36.
45. *Ibid.*, 41.

The following Figure 2 The total number of mobile telephone service accounts in Montenegro 2010–2022[46]) represents the total number of mobile telephone service accounts in Montenegro for the period of 2010 to 2022, along with the market penetration percentage.

Figure 2 The Total Number of Mobile Telephone Service Accounts in Montenegro 2010–2022

From a total of 1,274,031 mobile phone users in Montenegro at the end of 2022, the mobile operator with the most users was Mtel with 454,070 users, followed by Crnogorski Telekom with 448,848 users, and One Montenegro with 371,113 users, or in percentage, Mtel with 35.64%, Crnogorski Telekom with 35.23%, and One with 29.13%. Of the total number of 713,625 postpaid users, Crnogorski Telekom had 285,501, Mtel had 240,909, and One Montenegro had 187,215; Mtel had 213,161, One had 183,898, and Crnogorski Telekom had 163,347 prepaid users. The share of mobile operators among total users is represented in Figure 3.[47]

46. *Ibid.*, 42.
47. *Ibid.*

Figure 3 The Share of Mobile Operators Among Total Users

33. Users of Montenegro's three mobile providers generated a total of 1,955,719,253 minutes of outbound traffic in 2022. One Montenegro had the highest proportion of total outgoing traffic (37.07%), followed by Crnogorski Telekom (32.96%) and Mtel (29.97%).[48] Figure 4[49] shows the market shares of operators based on the amount of outbound traffic.

48. *Ibid.*, 43.
49. *Ibid.*, 44.

Figure 4 The Market Shares of Operators Based on the Amount of Outbound Traffic

34. In the domain of fixed broadband Internet connections, the number of users of mobile broadband access via data SIM cards rose by 9.04% in 2022 compared to 2021, while the number of people who accessed the Internet via mobile networks increased by 14.42% in December 2022 compared to December 2021.[50]

35. The penetration of fixed broadband access at the end of 2022 was 31.64% in relation to the number of inhabitants, while the penetration in relation to the number of households was 103.70%. The penetration of fixed broadband connections in relation to the number of households is significantly higher in relation to the availability of NGA for the reason that all Internet connections were taken into account since in the coastal and certain municipalities in the central part of Montenegro, the number of connections is significantly higher in relation to the number of households (e.g., in some coastal cities, more than two and a half connections per household were registered). The percentage of households in the NGA availability area (30 Mb/s) was 81.70%. Mobile broadband penetration, i.e., the number of users who accessed the Internet via mobile networks during December 2022, was 103.70%.[51]

36. Mtel and Telemach in Montenegro provide internet access by utilizing cable distribution systems, i.e., hybrid optical-coaxial (HFC-Hybrid Fiber-Coaxial) networks. Both operators have implemented the DOCSIS 3.0 protocol, which allows for high data transmission speeds. Total Internet traffic obtained by fixed electronic communication network users in 2022 was 518.41 PB, 47.02% more than in 2021.[52] In terms of mobile broadband connectivity, the total number of people who accessed the internet using data SIM cards rose by 9.04% in 2022 compared to 2021.[53]

50. *Ibid.*, 57.
51. *Ibid.*, 58.
52. *Ibid.*, 62.
53. *Ibid.*, 57.

37. In terms of mobile broadband access, the total number of people who accessed the Internet through their data SIM cards rose by 9.04% in 2022 compared to 2021 (Table 1: The total number of data SIM card users in Montenegro for the period 2015–2022.[54]

Table 1 The Total Number of Data SIM Card Users in Montenegro for the Period 2015–2022

	Data SIM Cards							
	2015	*2016*	*2017*	*2018*	*2019*	*2020*	*2021*	*2022*
Crnogorski Telekom	21.439	21.068	26.972	28.312	32.093	32.396	31.008	32.088
One Crna Gora	32.232	34.220	38.641	26.172	17.711	15.235	17.038	20.303
Total	53.671	55.288	65.613	54.484	49.804	47.631	48.046	52.391

38. Based on the latest reports, Crnogorski Telekom SIM card users generated 16.26 PB of bandwidth, representing a 36.67% progression from 2021. Users of One Montenegro attained traffic of 6.05 PB, representing a 10.12% growth over 2021.

39. The Internet penetration in the Montenegrin market in proportion to the number of inhabitants is indicated in Table 2, which represents the Internet penetration in the Montenegrin market in relation to the number of inhabitants.[55]

Table 2 The Internet Penetration in the Montenegrin Market in Relation to the Number of Inhabitants

	2015 (%)	*2016 (%)*	*2017 (%)*	*2018 (%)*	*2019 (%)*	*2020 (%)*	*2021 (%)*	*2022 (%)*
Fixed	18.1	18.5	22.2	25.0	28.8	29.7	30.4	31.6
Mobile	52.6	60.8	67.5	74.5	81.5	87.0	90.6	103.7

54. *Ibid.*, 68.
55. *Ibid.*

Chapter 4. E-Commerce: Facts and Figures

40. Rapid technological advancement and the increasing use of technology have created opportunities for conducting business electronically in Montenegro, as well as the conditions for the emergence of new business models. Despite the tremendous economic potential of e-commerce, especially in terms of significant reductions in product distribution costs, as a vital segment of the country's future economic development, it has been significantly reduced by long-standing barriers to internationalization in the form of a lack of globally recognized payment processors (e.g., Paypal). Namely, the lack of credible payment processors for the area of Montenegro has resulted in payment transactions via Paypal taking place in only one direction: from Montenegro to other countries, but not from other countries to Montenegro. This leads to a series of negative repercussions in terms of the undermined credibility of potential clients and investors in the national institutions of the system, requiring additional measures to improve the possibility of international payment transactions.

41. Notwithstanding the high level of ICT infrastructure development and well-developed Internet access at the national level, the general conclusion is that this resource is not utilized to its fullest extent for business purposes but rather for entertainment and social purposes. Although circumstances such as those during the COVID pandemic increased accessibility of online stores, special benefits such as discounts, harmonization of regulations, and consumer protection as an element accompanying online payments significantly contributed to the national growth trend of online commerce.

42. In Montenegro, there are no specialized studies on e-commerce, so limited data is only available through the private companies' periodical surveys and annual analysis of the national economy conducted by the Chamber of Commerce of Montenegro. According to the latest available report for 2022, 53% of respondents have never purchased or ordered products or services online; 74.5% of companies with a web presence stated that they provide access to product catalogs and price advertisements; and 65.0% have links to offers from their assortment on their social media profiles.[56]

43. The MasterIndex Montenegro survey is a traditional annual survey of the habits and needs of active payment card users in Montenegro. Based on the 2020 MasterIndex Montenegro survey, 17% of respondents attempted online payments for the first time during the pandemic period (this predominantly pertains to the consumer goods market, where customers are more willing to take risks with fresh food and beverage brands, a trend that is supported by the general rise in e-commerce grocery shopping). According to available data for the year 2022, the majority of

56. The Chamber of Commerce of Montenegro, https://komora.me/wp-content/uploads/2022/12/cg-privreda-2022.pdf, Mar. 23, 2023, 56.

online payments are done multiple times per year (34%), whereas 11% of respondents pay online at least once every week. According to the report, 69% of respondents used payment cards in e-commerce, and 41% paid in cash at pick-up. The majority of online payments are done multiple times per year (34%), whereas 11% of respondents pay online at least once every week. In accordance with the report, payment is made using all accessible payment methods, with 69% of respondents using payment cards in e-commerce and 41% paying in cash at pick-up. Online payments are primarily employed for purchases of clothing, shoes, and jewelry (39%). Additionally, respondents online buy home items (35%), pay monthly and other expenses (26%), buy sports equipment (20%), and utilize cards to pay for groceries (16%). Domestic web stores are more frequently visited than international internet retailers (34% versus 19% of respondents), and 7% had no preference.[57] The demographic characteristics regarding age and gender of the e-commerce consumers in Montenegro are showcased in Figure 5.[58]

57. Bankar.me, Mastercard Indeks Montenegro 2022, https://www.bankar.me/2022/06/08/masterindex-crna-gora-2022-65-odsto-ispitanika-karticama-placa-racune-do-40-eura/, Mar. 16, 2023.
58. Start.io, "E-Commerce in Montenegro," https://www.start.io/audience/e-commerce-consumers-in-montenegro, Feb. 17, 2023.

Figure 5 The Demographic Characteristics of the E-Commerce Consumers in Montenegro

44. Given that e-commerce is one of the most promising areas of trade in CEFTA[59] economies, it is expected that regional integration in this area will enhance Montenegro's comparative advantages and improve the free movement of goods while enabling access to new markets, a greater selection of products, more competitive prices, and lower transaction costs.

45. The EU4Business: Support for Regional Economic Integration initiative was launched in June 2022 with the goal of boosting CEFTA regional economic integration in the areas of quality infrastructure and internet commerce. This initiative is being implemented with the support of the German Federal Ministry for Economic Cooperation and Development (BMZ) and is an extension of the collaboration between the German government, the EU, and CEFTA signatories for the implementation of trade reforms within CEFTA. The project's main focus is on facilitating the implementation of the Action Plan for the Common Regional Market in the area of e-commerce, which anticipates that the Western Balkans' common market will be harmonized with EU legislation, bringing the region closer to the single EU market. This mechanism is expected to provide Montenegrin businesses and consumers with a significant reduction in business barriers, easier and safer electronic trade of goods, and protection against unfair competition, unsafe products, and excessive operating costs. As part of the project, the first regional e-commerce platform "E-commerce for All"[60] was launched for assessing the current situation of e-commerce in CEFTA markets through statistical data and interactive graphs on the state of e-commerce in each market alongside comparisons of customers, information on countries' readiness for e-commerce, etc. Based on realized data, Serbia and Kosovo have the highest percentage of online shoppers, followed by North Macedonia, Bosnia and Herzegovina, and Montenegro. Kosovo ranks highest in Europe, with 77% of online consumers buying garments over the Internet, followed by Montenegro (71%), while North Macedonia (57%), Bosnia and Herzegovina (56%), and Serbia (52%) fall below the European average. Figure 6 represents a summary of the most recent statistical data on e-commerce in Montenegro in comparison to other CEFTA countries.

59. The Central European Free Trade Agreement (CEFTA) presently consists of the Western Balkan economies of Albania, Bosnia and Herzegovina, Kosovo, Macedonia, Serbia, and Montenegro, in addition to Moldova. The CEFTA area has an overall population of approximately twenty million residents (Montenegro has the lowest population and Serbia has the highest), https://cefta.int, Feb. 14, 2023.

60. "E-commerce for All," www.ecommerce4all.eu, Feb. 12, 2023.

Figure 6 The Demographic Characteristics of the E-Commerce Consumers in Montenegro

Chapter 5. e-Government Initiatives

46. Montenegro has initiated a number of e-government initiatives designed to improve the delivery of public services, increase administrative efficiency, and facilitate digital transformation. E-government initiatives in Montenegro contributed significantly to national development, including improved administrative efficiency, enhanced service delivery, greater transparency and accountability, as well as economic and commercial growth.

47. The implementation of e-government in Montenegro entails the transformation of national industry, which includes not only the transformation of business processes involving interaction with citizens and business entities but also the transformation of Public Administration (PA) processes. The Ministry of Information Society of Montenegro conducted the first research on the degree of development of e-government initiatives at the national level at the end of 2009 as part of the implementation of the National Strategy for the Development of the Information Society for the period 2009 to 2013.[61] These initiatives streamlined administrative procedures, decreased bureaucratic red tape, and provided citizens and businesses with user-friendly online platforms to access government services. E-government initiatives possess the potential to accelerate the country's development by optimizing operational effectiveness, upgrading service delivery, promoting transparency, stimulating digital inclusion, encouraging data-driven decision-making, assisting in environmental long-term sustainability, and guaranteeing equal development opportunities for all. Detailed information regarding the most important e-government services is provided in Part II: Online public services. Other notable e-government initiatives in Montenegro are listed below:

At the beginning of June 2019, the system for measuring and analyzing the quality of the Internet access service "EKIP NetTest" was implemented. The EKIP NetTest system enables the measurement of Internet access service quality parameters in fixed and mobile electronic communication networks in Montenegro. EKIP NetTest is available at https://nettest.ekip.me/.

Montenegro has implemented an electronic procurement platform available at the web address: https://www.javne-nabavke.com/. The platform aims to digitize the public procurement process, enable legal entities to participate in tendering processes online, and provide greater transparency.

The application "Tariff Calculator" (kalkulator.ekip.me) provides assistance to users when choosing electronic communication services. The calculator has an informative character and is an interactive tool for comparing offers of public electronic communication services in Montenegro in the areas of fixed and mobile telephony, internet access services, distribution of TV and radio programs (AVM content), and other related services.

Register in electronic form in order to protect users from receiving unwanted messages and calls for the purpose of direct marketing, which contains phone

61. Vujica Lazovic, Tamara Djurickovic, "Economic Analysis of the e-Government Development in Montenegro," Montenegrin Journal of Economics No. 12, Vol. VI, 104.

numbers and e-mail addresses of users who do not want to receive such messages or calls. The register is available at the following web address: www.nezovime.ekip.me. By registering in the Register, the user chooses not to receive electronic messages and phone calls for the purpose of direct marketing and thereby withdraws all previously given consents.

48. In order to provide electronic communication operators and other subjects with the availability of data on electronic communication infrastructure, the AECPS has developed a Geoportal, which is available at http://geoportal.ekip.me. Through this portal, operators submit data about their electronic communication infrastructure, and the agency publishes this data on the Geoportal. The Geoportal contains data on the existing and planned infrastructure of the operators, as well as on the coverage of broadband Internet access by technology, speed, and number of operators that provide this service. This system is used by operators, processors of spatial planning documents, state, local, and other institutions, investors, and other interested natural and legal persons:

No	*Company Name*	*Registered Activity*	*Work Since*	*Operator Name Used in This Report*
1.	Crnogorski Telekom A.D. Podgorica	Communication networks and operators of public fixed electronic communication services: voice, sound, and image transmission (AVM), data transmission, fax, intelligent network services, public telephone booth services, leased line services, voice transmission service over Internet Protocol-based networks, callback service, value-added services, and any other fixed telecommunication services, as well as operator of public mobile electronic communication networks and operator of public mobile electronic communication services.	2009	Crnogorski Telekom

No	*Company Name*	*Registered Activity*	*Work Since*	*Operator Name Used in This Report*
2.	One Crna Gora d.o.o. Podgorica	Operator of public mobile electronic communication networks and operator of public mobile electronic communication services, public fixed electronic communication networks, public fixed electronic communication services, and electronic communication infrastructure leasing services.	2009	One Crna Gora
3.	Mtel d.o.o. Podgorica	Operator of publicly available telephone services in a fixed electronic communication network, publicly available services in a mobile electronic communication network, transmission and distribution services of audio-visual media content, public electronic communication multiplexing services, transmission of multiplexed signals to the transmitter multiplex network for broadcasting radio-diffusion and other signals, internet access services, data transmission services, and leased line services.	2009	Mtel

No	*Company Name*	*Registered Activity*	*Work Since*	*Operator Name Used in This Report*
4.	Telemach d.o.o. Podgorica	Operator of public fixed electronic communication networks and operator of public fixed electronic communication services: internet access, fixed telephony, distribution of audio-visual media content, and voice transmission services over the internet (VoIP).	2009	Telemach
5.	Wimax Montenegro d.o.o. Podgorica	Operator of public electronic communication network based on broadband wireless access (BWA) and operator of public electronic communication services.	2009	Wimax Montenegro
6.	Radio-difuzni centar d.o.o. Podgorica	Operator of public electronic communication network for transmission and broadcasting of radio-diffusion and other signals, public electronic communication services for transmission and broadcasting of radio-diffusion signals, public electronic communication services for leased lines, public electronic communication services for multiplexing and transmission of multiplexed signals to the transmitter multiplex network for broadcasting radio-diffusion and other signals, and electronic communication infrastructure leasing services.	2009.	Radio-difuzni centar

No	*Company Name*	*Registered Activity*	*Work Since*	*Operator Name Used in This Report*
7.	Pošta Crne Gore A.D. Podgorica	Operator of public fixed electronic communication network and operator of public fixed electronic communication services for providing public service of public telephone booths and providing public service of voice transmission over Internet Protocol-based networks.	2009	Pošta Crne Gore
8.	Radio Euro Taxi d.o.o. Bar	Operator of public electronic communication services through its own functional network/system.	2009	Radio Euro taxi
9.	Orion Telekom d.o.o. Podgorica	Operator of publicly available telephone services in a fixed electronic communication network, transmission and distribution services of audio-visual media content (excluding terrestrial radio broadcasting), voice transmission services over the internet, internet access services, data transmission services, value-added services, and SMS services.	2010	Orion Telekom
10.	Ipmont d.o.o. Podgorica	Operator of public electronic communication services: voice transmission over Internet Protocol-based networks (operator selection and preselection, prepaid calling cards, Call Shop, and SIP users), internet access services, leased line services, and access and usage of electronic communication network elements (optical fiber leasing—Dark Fiber).	2010	Ipmont

No	*Company Name*	*Registered Activity*	*Work Since*	*Operator Name Used in This Report*
11.	Crnogorski Elektoprenosni Sistem Podgorica	Operator of public fixed electronic communication network and operator of public fixed electronic communication services for providing optical fiber leasing services (Dark Fiber).	2010	CGES
12.	Satellite Broadband Service Network Montenegro d.o.o. Podgorica	Operator of public electronic communication networks and services, operator of public satellite electronic communication services for providing public internet access services and leased line services.	2011	SBS Net Montenegro
13.	Wireless Montenegro d.o.o. Podgorica	Operator of public electronic communication networks based on the TETRA (Terrestrial Trunked Radio) standard and electronic communication services for voice and short text message transmission via TETRA system and internet access services.	2012	Wireless Montenegro
14.	Siol d.o.o. Podgorica	Operator of public fixed electronic communication network and operator of public fixed electronic communication services for internet access services, leased line services, and access and usage of electronic communication network elements (optical fiber leasing).	2012	Siol
15.	Komunalne usluge d.o.o. Podgorica	Operator providing optical fiber leasing services (Dark Fiber) and electronic communication infrastructure leasing services.	2012	Komunalne usluge

No	*Company Name*	*Registered Activity*	*Work Since*	*Operator Name Used in This Report*
16.	Cogent Communications Montenegro d.o.o. Podgorica	Operator of public electronic communication access to the internet, Ethernet connections (point-to-point), and IP transit.	2013	Cogent Communications Montenegro
17.	Lona Trade d.o.o. Ulcinj	Operator of public electronic communication access to the internet.	2013	Lona Trade
18.	CPA d.o.o. Podgorica	Operator providing optical fiber leasing services (Dark Fiber) and electronic communication infrastructure leasing.	2014	CPA
19.	Fibercom d.o.o. Podgorica	Operator of public electronic communication access to the internet, leased lines, and optical fiber leasing (Dark Fiber). Operator of public fixed electronic communication network for services: publicly available telephone services in a fixed electronic communication network, internet access services, and transmission and distribution services of audio-visual media content (excluding terrestrial radio broadcasting).	2015	FiberCom
20.	Teleeye-Montenegro	Operator of public fixed electronic communication network (fixed wireless access at 5GHz) for internet access services.	2015	Teleeye Montenegro
21.	Željeznicka infrastruktura Crne Gore A.D. Poodgorica	Operator of public electronic communication services for access and usage of electronic communication network elements and electronic communication infrastructure leasing services.	2016	ŽICG

No	*Company Name*	*Registered Activity*	*Work Since*	*Operator Name Used in This Report*
22.	Univerzitet Crne Gore – CIS Podgorica	Operator of public electronic communication services for connection to the national internet exchange point (IXP).	2016	Univerzitet Crne Gore – CIS
23	Aquaterra solutions d.o.o. Budva	Operator of public electronic communication services for internet access	2016	Aquaterra Solutions
24	Crnogorski elektodistributivni sistem d.o.o. Podgorica	Operator of public electronic communication services for issuing optical fibers and leasing electronic communication infrastructure.	2017	CEDIS
25	MDS Network d.o.o. Tuzi	Operator of public electronic communication services for internet access.	2017	MDS Network
26	ASP CO d.o.o. Herceg Novi	Operator of public electronic communication services for internet access.	2017	ASP CO
27	INFO SISTEMI d.o.o. Podgorica	Operator of public electronic communication services for internet access, data transmission, and optical fiber leasing.	2018	Info sistemi
28	NETMONT d.o.o. Bar	Operator of public electronic communication services for internet access.	2018	NetMont
29	SIMES NET d.o.o. Podgorica	Operator of public electronic communication services in a fixed electronic communication network for transmission and distribution of audio-visual media content, internet access, leased lines, optical fiber leasing (Dark Fiber), and leasing of electronic communication infrastructure.	2019	Simes Net

No	*Company Name*	*Registered Activity*	*Work Since*	*Operator Name Used in This Report*
30	RTV Mir&Teuta d.o.o. Ulcinj	Operator of public electronic communication services for access to digital terrestrial radio broadcasting multiplex and transmission and/or broadcasting of audio-visual media content and other data intended for direct reception in terrestrial broadcasting.	2020.	RTV Mir&Teuta
31	RED d.o.o. Podgorica	Operator of public electronic communication services through its own functional network/ system.	2021	RED
32	Regionalni Vodovod Crnogorsko Primorje d.o.o. Budva	Operator of public electronic communication services for providing optical fiber leasing services (Dark Fiber).	2021	Regionalni vodovod Crnogorsko primorje
33	Portonovi Resort Management Company d.o.o. Kumbor	Operator of public electronic communication services for providing optical fiber leasing services (Dark Fiber) and leasing of electronic communication infrastructure.	2021	Portonovi Resort Management Company
34	Pro Solutions d.o.o. Tivat	Operator of public electronic communication services for internet access.	2022	Pro Solutions

Part I. Digital Market Regulation

Chapter 1. Legal Status of Standards and Technical Specifications (Non-binding Self-Regulation)

49. Montenegro's ICT development approach is aligned with European strategies (EU Digital Agenda, Digital Agenda and for the Western Balkans, Strategy for the Single Digital Market, and European Compass 2030), as well as national strategies:

- Digital Transformation Strategy 2022–2026.
- Smart Specialization Strategy 2019–2024.
- Sustainable Development Strategy 2016–2030.
- Cybersecurity Strategy 2022–2026.

50. The Digital Transformation Strategy of Montenegro 2022–2026[62] is the overarching strategic framework of digital transformation that defines the prerequisites and required initiatives for digital transformation and the proactive development of digital Montenegro. The strategy provides a comprehensive overview of the organizational, legal, technical, and social aspects of digital transformation, as well as the process's most significant challenges. That is supported by concrete data and information in individual segments (organization, e-services, eID, trust in ICT, interoperability, skills and education, coordination of ICT industries) that result in beneficial effects on revenue generation, improve the welfare of society as a whole, and ultimately have a positive impact on the advancement of the economy.

51. Montenegro addresses the challenges of its digital transformation through two strategic goals:

(1) Enhancement of resources and capabilities for Montenegro's digital transformation, within which four operational objectives have been identified:
   - Innovative and effective coordination and monitoring of digital transformation.
   - Enhancing availability, interoperability, and data management.
   - Broader coverage and modernization of the electronic communication infrastructure.

62. The Digital Transformation Strategy of Montenegro 2022–2026, https://www.gov.me/en/documents/59dcab9b-b0e8-48b7-830b-6e4eab690521, May 27, 2023.

  - Development and improvement of digital skills and expertise within the Montenegrin population.
- (2) Increasing the digital awareness of the Montenegrin population and the digital competitiveness of the ICT sector, with three operational objectives:
  - Increasing both citizens' and enterprises' awareness of the significance of digital development.
  - Enhancing the quality, quantity, and accessibility of e-services.
  - Increasing and developing the ICT sector.

52. Within the operational objective, increased coverage and modernization of the information and telecommunications infrastructure, the implementation of a high level of 5G network coverage, and increased Internet access are projected as key activities.

53. Montenegro was the first non-EU country to implement the Smart Specialization Strategy (S3)[63] in June 2019, despite the fact that it was not a requirement of its accession negotiations. S3 is focused on strengthening the country's comparative advantages by encouraging innovation in applied research and strengthening collaborative connections between the private, public, and nonprofit sectors. This strategy is based on the analysis of the national economy's requirements and potential through the so-called entrepreneurial discovery process, with the participation of numerous interested parties.

54. Priorities for the development of Montenegro were selected in four areas:

(1) energy and sustainable environment;
(2) sustainable agriculture and food value chain;
(3) health tourism;
(4) information and communication technologies.

55. Within the selected priority areas, emphasis is placed on ICT as a key instrument for enhancing national competitiveness and as the only horizontal sector that provides support and creates prerequisites for the sustainable development of all other sectors. The strategy stipulates that the development of ICT in Montenegro will take place through the implementation of key reforms regarding fostering the digital economy and enhancing the ICT industry's competitiveness through innovative activities.[64]

---

63. Smart Specialization Strategy of Montenegro (S3) 2019–2024, https://www.gov.me/dokumenta/18205a91-1afc-4eb7-a5cb-8ad5bd0b7712, Jan. 30, 2023.
64. According to Regulation 1059/2003 of the European Commission, based on its area and population, Montenegro is defined as one NUTS4 region, which implies that it is regarded as a single region. https://s3.me/pametna-specijalizacija-u-crnoj-gori/, Jan. 30, 2023.

56. Following the global adoption of the UN's Agenda 2030 in 2015, Montenegro enacted the National Strategy for Sustainable Development 2016–2030[65] as a long-term strategic document for the country's development. In Montenegro, particularly, the expansion of the ICT infrastructure is a prerequisite for reducing regional imbalances and supporting the economic growth of the northern region. Within the thematic area of Natural Resources—preserving natural capital, the Strategy sets as one of the key objectives the addressing of unsustainable spatial capacity issues, including 9.c.1 indicator: the share of the population covered by the mobile network, by technology. In Montenegro, particularly, the expansion of the information and communication infrastructure is a prerequisite for decreasing regional imbalances and supporting the economic growth of the northern region. As key sub-measures pertaining to ICT, the strategy stipulates the continued growth of broadband Internet access, enhancing the level of governance's transparency, and expanding the e-government portal as the central web window for administration services at both the local and national levels for providing electronic data and encourage electronic participation.[66]

57. In terms of information security, Montenegro adopted its first national cybersecurity strategy in 2013, outlining guidelines for developing national capacities (legislative, operational, human, financial, and technical) to properly respond to cyberspace challenges and threats. The Cybersecurity Strategy for the period 2022–2026[67] is currently being implemented at the national level (further information on the Cybersecurity Strategy is provided in Part V).

58. The Accession Program of Montenegro to the European Union for the period 2022–2023[68] within Chapter 10: Information Society and Media addresses three areas: electronic communications, information society services, and audiovisual policy. Core electronic communications themes encompass broadband internet access, standardization, interconnection, business market analysis, universal service, the rights of customers, privacy concerns, digitization, and radio spectrum policy. The Montenegro Progress Report for 2022 defines key legislative recommendations, such as harmonization with EU legal acquis on electronic communications and information technologies, including the European Electronic Communications Code, Network and Information Security Directive, 5G Cybersecurity Toolbox, Open Data Directive, and ePrivacy Directive. One of the planned measures within Chapter 10 is the adoption of the Strategy for the Introduction of 5G Mobile Communication Networks in Montenegro.

---

65. National Strategy for Sustainable Development 2016–2030, https://www.gov.me/dokumenta/67dc487e-097d-41d2-8fd5-7827a19a1f5a, Jan. 3, 2023.
66. Javne politike, "Information and communication technologies: Sustainable development goals and international commitments," https://javnepolitike.me/en/policy/information-and-communication-technologies/, Mar. 12, 2023.
67. Cybersecurity Strategy of Montenegro 2022–2026, https://www.gov.me/dokumenta/85e2a9d0-0d3c-483a-9822-515d3b7798de, Mar. 23, 2023.
68. The Accession Program of Montenegro to the European Union for the period 2022–2023, https://www.eu.me/wpfd_file/program-pristupanja-crne-gore-evropskoj-uniji-2022-2023/, Jan. 29, 2023.

59. In November 2020, the Western Balkan countries signed a Memorandum of understanding on the 5G roadmap for digital transformation and on regional interoperability and trust services in the region.[69] The objective of the memorandum is to raise awareness about the digital transformation of citizens in the region and reinforce regional cooperation and assistance. The memorandum identifies four fundamental domains: network and service connectivity, trust and security, digital skills, and the digital economy. In order to accomplish digital transformation, significant investments and measures facilitating 5G service coverage and accessibility for all citizens are required. As a signatory to the Memorandum, Montenegro has taken initiatives to align policies, regulations, and technical measures to support private initiatives, encourage investments, ensure a sustainable competitive environment, and promote best practices. In alignment with that, in December 2021, the Government of Montenegro adopted the Roadmap for the deployment of 5G networks and broadband infrastructure development in Montenegro,[70] which specifies actions and reforms for the development of 5G networks.

60. The Program of Economic Reforms 2023–2025[71] is a key economic policy document in Montenegro that outlines a set of measures and structural reforms for reaching smart, sustainable, and inclusive economic development. Within the Program, Reform Measure 11 aims to further strengthen the legislative and regulatory system for the continued development of broadband internet access infrastructure to guarantee the availability of broadband communication networks and services. As part of this measure, the endorsement of the 5G Network Development Strategy in Montenegro and the development of an Action plan for enacting this strategy are scheduled. The primary goal of the Strategy for the development of 5G mobile communication networks is to attain higher standards of service along with the enhancement of ICT in Montenegro, as well as to establish the country's strategic directions in this area. The Action Plan 2023–2025 is an integral part of the Strategy for the Development of 5G in Montenegro and incorporates measurable performance and result indicators, whose evaluation and tracking enable a systematic monitoring process to conduct an accurate assessment of strategic objectives. On the basis of the Development Strategy of the Information Society of Montenegro, a Migration plan to the Ipv6 protocol was developed with the primary goal of addressing the Ipv4 protocol's Internet address shortage. In addition to the enlargement of the address domain, this protocol provides greater utility, protection, and the ability to deploy modern IoT solutions. Considering that public institutions and local authorities are among the largest consumers of ICT resources in Montenegro and the migration to

---

69. EUROACTIV, "Digital transformation and connectivity key for Western Balkans," https://www.euractiv.com/section/politics/short_news/digital-transformation-and-connectivity-key-for-western-balkans/, May 7, 2022.
70. Roadmap for deployment of 5G networks and broadband infrastructure development in Montenegro, https://www.gov.me/en/article/roadmap-for-deployment-of-5g-networks-and-broadband-infrastructure-development, Dec. 12, 2022.
71. The Program of Economic Reforms 2023–2025 for Montenegro, https://www.gov.me/dokumenta/da1d441a-47a6-4245-a156-c94602f21ab6, Jan. 22, 2023.

Ipv6 is a state-level strategic objective, it was necessary to propose and emphasize the migration plan separately for this group of subjects. Several recommendations were put forward according to the plan:

– Formation of a national body ("Ipv6 task force") tasked with creating an action plan for the migration of state institutions to Ipv6, coordinating activities, promoting, and monitoring the migration process.
– Supporting and coordinating promotion of the benefits of the Ipv6 protocol and education on subject migration strategies at all levels of PA and among residential users.
– Establish a laboratory within the University of Montenegro's Central Information System for assessing the transition to Ipv6.
– Formulation of Ipv6 recommendations and guidelines for state institutions.[72]

61. At the national level, actions have been taken to implement the principles of Net Neutrality to guarantee the equal and non-discriminatory treatment of internet traffic and related user rights. Since Montenegro is not a member of the EU, Regulation 2015/2120 of the European Parliament and Council is not directly applicable; therefore, amendments to national law are required for its implementation. However, this has not yet been accomplished, so the current LEC of Montenegro does not contain any provisions imposed by this Regulation.

72. Agency for Electronic Communications and Postal Services, "Migration Plan to the IPv6 Protocol in Montenegro," https://www.ekip.me/latest-informations/announcement/plan-migracije-na-protokol-ipv6-u-crnoj-gori, Jan. 12, 2023.

Chapter 2. Legal Status of Standard Terms and Conditions

62. The substantial investments made in the electronic communications industry are a demonstration of Montenegro's sound regulatory environment, which guarantees fair conditions for all market players and promotes competition as the best form of regulation. The digital market in Montenegro is primarily governed by the Law on Electronic Communications ("Official Gazette of Montenegro," Nos. 40/13, 56/13, 2/17, and 49/19), adopted in 2013. Based on public consultation processes run by the AECPS of Montenegro, the law has already undergone three amendments. The regulations in Montenegro governing the provision of Universal Service in electronic communications are based on Directive (EU) 2002/22/EC of the European Parliament and Council of March 7, 2002, on Universal Service and Users' Rights Relating to Electronic Communications Networks and Services (Universal Service Directive) and Directive 2009/136/EC of the European Parliament and Council of November 25, 2009.

63. In addition to the LEC, the Agency, the Ministry of Economic Development, the Ministry of Finance and Social Welfare, and the Government of Montenegro have all adopted secondary legislation that governs the delivery of universal service in electronic communications. These include:

- regulation on the Minimum Set of Services Covered by Universal Service ("Official Gazette of Montenegro," Nos. 46/14 and 72/20);
- rulebook on the Quality of Universal Service ("Official Gazette of Montenegro," No. 23/14);
- rulebook on Types of Benefits and Special Measures for Access to Public Electronic Communication Services for Persons with Disabilities ("Official Gazette of Montenegro," Nos. 43/14 and 26/17);
- rulebook on Determining Data Transmission Speed for Functional Internet Access via Universal Service ("Official Gazette of Montenegro," Nos. 46/14 and 80/18);
- rulebook on Determining the List of Categories of Users with Special Benefits in Using Universal Service ("Official Gazette of Montenegro," Nos. 52/14 and 75/15);
- rulebook on Criteria for Assessing the Justifiability of User Requests for Access to Public Electronic Communication Networks via Universal Service ("Official Gazette of Montenegro," No. 56/13);
- rulebook on the Methodology for Calculating the Net Cost of Providing Universal Service ("Official Gazette of Montenegro," Nos. 12/14 and 101/20); Rulebook on the Method of Assessing the Accessibility of Prices for Services and Special Packages of Universal Service for Socially Vulnerable Persons and Persons with Disabilities ("Official Gazette of Montenegro," Nos. 33/14 and 13/17); and
- rulebook on the Implementation of Public Tenders and Conditions for Designating Universal Service Operators ("Official Gazette of Montenegro," No. 45/14.

64. The activity of electronic communications and management and use of limited resources in Montenegro are based on the following principles:

(1) equality of opportunity, objectivity, and transparency;
(2) providing favorable market conditions for electronic communications to continue growing sustainably throughout Montenegro;
(3) ensuring that the business environment is reliable and that company operators are treated equally;
(4) aligning ICT operations with international and domestic standards;
(5) ensuring that universal services are accessible to all residents of Montenegro and in accordance with their needs, particularly those of people with disabilities and socially disadvantaged users;
(6) guaranteeing fair and mutually accepted agreements for the interconnection of electronic communications networks and services;
(7) protecting and encouraging competition in the market for electronic communications in order to ensure user advantages;
(8) encouraging effective resource management and use;
(9) providing benefits for users, especially those with limited mobility, those with disabilities, the elderly, and people who are socially vulnerable, with respect to the preference, expenditure, terms for access and usage, and the overall quality of electronic communications services;
(10) facilitating a swift and efficient dispute resolution process to ensure user safety in their interactions with operators;
(11) fostering innovations, investments, and the creation of a new and upgraded infrastructure;
(12) gradual improvement of electronic communications service quality;
(13) guaranteeing the privacy and protection of personal information;
(14) enabling end users the option to freely access and disseminate information or utilize apps and services of their own selection while utilizing public communication networks and services;
(15) securing the reliability and integrity of public electronic telecommunications networks;
(16) maintaining a system for providing users with accurate and timely information about the costs and terms of using such services; and
(17) guaranteeing the protection of users' interests.[73]

65. In December 2017, the Rulebook on the Quality of Public Electronic Communication Services from 2014 was replaced by the Rulebook on the Quality of Public Electronic Communication Services (Official Gazette of Montenegro, No. 002/2018). The Rulebook prescribes the parameters of the quality of public electronic communication services in fixed and mobile networks, as well as measurement methods, the method of publishing measurement results, and the time periods in which measurements are performed. In addition, it has been supplemented by a

73. Article 3 of the Law of Electronic Communication of Montenegro.

set of parameters for the availability and signal quality of digital terrestrial broadcasting systems for broadcasting second-generation television programs.

66. The Rulebook on Access and Interconnection ("Official Gazette of Montenegro" No. 24/14) is in accordance with the relevant Directives of the European Commission (Directive 2002/19/EC and Directive 2009/140/EC). The Rulebook prescribes in detail the basic goals and requirements for achieving access and interconnection, the procedure for submitting requests and responding to requests, their contents, deadlines for action in certain phases of the access and interconnection implementation procedure, as well as the conditions under which access and interconnection can be restricted.

67. The Regulation on the contents of the plan of measures to ensure the integrity of public electronic communication networks and the use of electronic communication services in emergency situations ("Official Gazette of Montenegro," No. 50/14) adopted by the Government of Montenegro in 2014 governs measures to ensure the security and integrity of electronic communication networks and services. On the basis of the Regulation, the Rulebook on the method and deadlines for the implementation of measures of security and integrity of electronic communication networks and services was adopted ("Official Gazette of Montenegro," Nos. 41/15 and 81/16), which prescribes the appropriate safety standards and measures in the following areas:

- Risk management.
- Security of human resources.
- Security of systems and facilities.
- Operations management.
- Incident management.
- Business continuity management.
- Monitoring, auditing, and testing.

68. The Parliament approved the Law on the Use of Physical Infrastructure for the Installation of High-Speed Electronic Communications (Official Gazette of Montenegro No. 001/22) in December 2021, consequently aligning with the EU Broadband Cost Reduction Directive. Nonetheless, Montenegro is required to finalize its compliance with the EU's electronic communications and information technology acquis. For the purpose of aligning the regulatory framework in the field of electronic communications with EU regulations, the Work Program of the Government of Montenegro for 2023 prescribes the establishment of a new LEC, which will transpose Directive 2018/1972/EU alongside EU Directive 2014/61, which regulates the operation of the physical infrastructure adapted for high-speed networks. In addition, the objective of drafting the new law is to promote the development of electronic communications networks and services in Montenegro and thus economic and social development in the country, including the development of the information society, ensuring access and use of high-speed networks for all citizens and businesses, and increasing the security of public electronic communication networks and services, particularly from a critical infrastructure (CI) standpoint.

69. As a component of its international activities, Montenegro has established cooperation with the leading global organizations in the field of electronic communications, such as the International Telecommunication Union (ITU), the Body of European Regulators in the Field of Electronic Communications (BEREC), the Conference of European Post and Telecommunications Administrations (CEPT), and the European Mediterranean regulatory group for electronic communications.

Chapter 3. International Private Law Applied to the Online Environment

70. International private law in Montenegro includes several sources that may be divided into three categories: domestic positive law, multilateral international agreements, and bilateral agreements.

71. The Private International Law (PIL) Act ("Official Gazette of Montenegro," No. 1/2014) is the main legislation of international private law in Montenegro. PIL determines the regulations for determining applicable law in private law issues with international implications ("conflict provisions"), the rules for judicial and other authorities' jurisdiction regarding such proceedings, the requirements for the procedure, and the norms for the recognition and enforcement of foreign judgments and arbitration awards, as well as decisions of other authorities.[74]

72. Multilateral international treaties that adhere to Montenegro include: conventions adopted under the auspices of the Hague Conference on PIL, conventions on international commercial arbitration (the European Convention on International Commercial Arbitration from 1961, the New York Convention on the Recognition and Enforcement of Foreign Arbitral Awards from 1958, and the Washington Convention on the Settlement of Investment Disputes between States and Nationals of Other States from 1989).

73. Bilateral agreements in the field of international private law have many aspects and primarily address the areas of international legal aid, recognition and enforcement of foreign decisions, protection of foreign investments, and information sharing.

74. The Law on PIL does not contain specific provisions related to the online environment; it stipulates that the interpretation and application of provisions related to contractual and non-contractual obligations shall be carried out in accordance with the Rome I Regulation (EC) No. 593/2008 and the Rome II Regulation (EC) No. 864/2007.

74. Article 1 of the The Private International Law Act of Montenegro ("Official Gazette of Montenegro," No. 1/2014).

Chapter 4. Competition Law Applied to the Digital Market

75. The ultimate objective of market regulation is to create effective competition in the electronic communications market so that consumers are able to select between multiple service providers, resulting in better and more affordable services that promote the market's subsequent progress. The Agency will collaborate with the organization in charge of competition protection in the procedure for identifying, monitoring, and analyzing relevant markets in the Montenegrin electronic communications market.

76. The "relevant market," according to LEC, is one that has structural, regulatory, and other long-term impediments that prohibit new competitors from entering the market and where it is difficult to create competition without *ex ante* intervention.[75]

77. Other markets may be subject to *ex ante* regulation if the Agency determines that they meet the following conditions:

(1) the presence of strong and long-lasting structural, legal, and regulatory barriers that prevent market entry;
(2) the market structure does not demonstrate tendencies to develop efficient market competition in a reasonable time frame; and
(3) changes in regulations governing competition protection do not provide an efficient reduction of market shortcomings.[76]

78. To prevent market discrimination and monitor the profitability of specific market segments, the agency conducts market analysis, identifies operators with Significant Market Power (SMP), and implements regulatory measures to mitigate the negative effects of SMP. An operator is considered to have considerable market power if, either individually or collectively with other operators, it has a position of economic dominance that allows it to act independently of competitors and users to a large extent. If two or more operators operate within the market structure that is regarded as enabling coordinated activities, they have been determined to have joint dominance in terms of economic power.[77] In determining the operator's significant market influence, the Agency is allowed to apply any of the following criteria:

(1) "market share of the operator in the relevant market and changes in structure for a longer period of time;
(2) barriers to entry into a relevant market and effects of potential competition on such a market;
(3) the influence of large users on the operators' power (countervailing purchase power);
(4) lack of potential competition;

75. Article 63 of the Law of Electronic Communication of Montenegro.
76. Article 65 of the Law of Electronic Communication of Montenegro.
77. Article 67 of the Law on Electronic Communications of Montenegro.

(5) economies of scale and economies of scope;
(6) technological advantages or superiority;
(7) development of sales and distribution networks;
(8) level of vertical integration;
(9) level of product diversification;
(10) privileged access to capital markets and financial resources;
(11) barriers to expansion;
(12) connection of provided services."[78]

79. The agency may request the SMP operator to:

(1) "negotiate in good faith with operators on requests for access to and use of network elements;
(2) enable access to specified network elements and/or facilities that are not active and/or access to the local loop for enabling carrier selection and/or carrier pre-selection and/or subscriber line resale offers;
(3) carry out the interconnection of electronic communications networks;
(4) not withdraw the access already granted;
(5) provide specified services on a wholesale basis because of the resale of those services on the retail market;
(6) grant free access to technical interfaces, protocols, and other technologies and possibilities that are indispensable for the interoperability of services and/or networks, including virtual network services;
(7) provide common accommodation of equipment and other forms of common usage of electronic communication infrastructure and related equipment;
(8) provide facilities necessary for interoperability of services for end users, including intelligent network services, distribution systems, or roaming services in mobile networks;
(9) provide access to operational support systems or similar systems necessary to ensure fair competition in the provision of services;
(10) provide access to related services, such as services based on data on the identity, location, and availability of users."[79]

78. Article 68 of the Law on Electronic Communications of Montenegro.
79. Article 75 of the Law on Electronic Communications of Montenegro.

Chapter 5. Regulation of the Electronic Communications Market ("Telecommunications Law")

80. The Agency for Electronic Communications and Postal Services (hereinafter "the Agency")[80] is responsible for the regulation of the Montenegrin electronic communication market. The Agency was established by the Government of Montenegro on March 8, 2001, as a regulatory authority for electronic communications and postal services on a national level. The Agency operates independently from all entities that utilize electronic communications networks, provide equipment or services on the markets for electronic communications and postal services, and provide equipment or services on the markets for postal services. The Agency's operations are regulated by the LEC[81] and the Law on Postal Services.[82] The Agency's administrative duties in the electronic communications sector are subject to the fundamental concepts of: establishing a secure and reliable business setting for the operators and their financial investments; implementing conditions for the implementation and growth of new technologies across all of the territory of Montenegro; supporting rationally employing limited resources (radio frequencies and numbers/addresses); and stimulating competitiveness. The Agency's activities are transparent, and all of its regulations are published in the "Official Gazette of Montenegro" and on its website. The Agency's Annual Report and Financial Report must be submitted to the Montenegrin Parliament for confirmation.

81. Article 11 of the LEC defines the Agency's competencies as follows:

(1) establishes regulations based on the authorizations stated by law;
(2) adopts and supervises the implementation of the Addressing Plan and Numbering Plan;
(3) prepares the recommended plan for spectrum allocation and monitors its implementation;
(4) supervises and manages the enforcement of Radio Frequency Assignment Plans;
(5) provides frameworks for the regulations that are approved by the Government and the Ministry;
(6) regulates and monitors the radio-frequency spectrum;
(7) undertakes initiatives towards guaranteeing the management of limited resources;
(8) governs the utilization of radio frequencies with international bodies and/or organizations;
(9) supports the national use of electronic communication infrastructure in accordance with the law;
(10) implements nondiscriminatory procedures for allocating limited resources;
(11) provides permissions for the use of limited resources;

80. The Agency for Electronic Communications and Postal Services, https://ekip.me/, Jun. 12, 2022.
81. Law on Electronic Communications ("Official Gazette of Montenegro," Nos. 40/13, 56/13, 2/17, and 49/19).
82. Law on Postal Services ("Official Gazette of Montenegro," Nos. 57/11, 55/16, and 55/18).

(12) manages the registers and databases in accordance with the law;
(13) establishes the amount of fees payable to the Agency by legal and natural entities in accordance with the law;
(14) resolves complaints from users, considers initiatives, and determines the procedure for protecting users' interests and rights;
(15) arbitrates disputes on the market for electronic communications;
(16) oversees the development and appoints the Universal Service operator;
(17) frequently publishes market development indicator data in accordance with the law;
(18) analyzes relevant markets, identifies operators with significant influence on the market, and implements regulatory measures to prevent the negative effects of operators' market power;
(19) performs professional supervision of the work of operators in accordance with Montenegrin law, technical regulations, and standards;
(20) performs professional supervision of the performance of operators' obligations in emergency situations;
(21) cooperates with regulatory bodies of other countries and, within its competences, participates in the work of managing and working bodies of competent European and international organizations and institutions in the field of electronic communications;
(22) conducts market and public opinion analyses and open consultative procedures in line with the law;
(23) performs other activities stipulated by the law.[83]

82. In the field of electronic communications, the Government of Montenegro:

(1) outlines a national strategy for the development of electronic communications and provides guidelines for its implementation;
(2) approves the plan for the allocation of radio frequency spectrum;
(3) provides an assessment to the Montenegrin Parliament on the Agency's financial report and business strategy with an accounting plan;
(4) determine the minimal set of services that must be provided by the Universal Service;
(5) specify the conditions under which electronic communications networks may be used in the event of an emergency; and
(6) perform other tasks stipulated by law.[84]

83. The Ministry of Economic Development and Tourism of Montenegro was established with the formation of the new government structure on April 28, 2022, with the following electronic communications-related responsibilities:

(1) coordinates procedures that promote the development of electronic communications;

---

83. Article 11 of the Law on Electronic Communications of Montenegro.
84. Article 5 of the Law on Electronic Communications of Montenegro.

(2) supervises the implementation of the electronic communications development policies;
(3) cooperates with the Agency and relevant administration bodies regarding the usage of radio-frequencies and electronic communications networks of importance for defense and security;
(4) supervises and executes the Government's decisions regarding requirements for using electronic communications networks and services in emergency situations;
(5) represents Montenegro in European and international organizations and institutions in matters of electronic communications;
(6) contributes to the activities of administrative and operational bodies of international organizations;
(7) carries out additional tasks imposed by law.[85]

84. The LEC defines electronic communications infrastructure and associated facilities as: "the infrastructure and facilities associated with an electronic communications network or electronic communications service that enables or supports service provision or can be used for service provision, including buildings or entrances thereto, cable ducts and lines in buildings, antennas and other masts, supporting structures, pipes, and canals, shafts and distribution cabinets and conditional access systems and related services."[86]

85. For the purposes of this LEC, an operator is defined as a natural or legal person and/or entrepreneur who provides or is authorized to provide a publicly accessible electronic communications service or enables the utilization of a public electronic communications network or public electronic communications infrastructure and related resources.[87]

86. The law stipulates that in order to convey signals by wire, radio, optical, or other electromagnetic systems, including satellite networks, fixed networks (with circuit and packet switching, including the Internet), electric power cable systems for signal transmission, and other resources, including passive network elements, the electronic communications network must include transmission systems. A network of electronic communications that is used only or primarily for transmitting data between network-ending nodes in addition to offering publicly accessible electronic communications services is referred to as a public network of electronic communications. The LEC defines an electronic communications service as a service that is generally provided for a fee and includes primarily or completely the transmission of signals via electronic communications networks involving telecommunications services and the service of broadcasting media. This excludes media-related service provision, editorial oversight of media content, and information society services transmitted via electronic communications networks. In accordance

85. Article 7 of the Law on Electronic Communications of Montenegro.
86. Article 36 of the Law on Electronic Communications of Montenegro.
87. Article 46 of the Law on Electronic Communications of Montenegro.

with the LEC, any electronic communications service provided within market terms is considered a publicly accessible electronic communications service.[88]

87. Electronic communications networks, electronic communications infrastructure, and their corresponding features must be constructed, generated, maintained, and used in alignment with the domestic and international standards as well as technical specifications applicable in Montenegro in a manner that safeguards:

(1) that doesn't interfere with the operation of other electronic communications systems, electronic communications infrastructure, and related services;
(2) accessibility of publicly available electronic communications services for people with disabilities.[89]

88. To ensure that the public has access to information regarding the quality of services provided by operators in Montenegro, operators are required to make electronic communications services of a prescribed quality and subscriber agreement available to the public. Following this, the Agency regularly publishes a comparative evaluation of quality parameters for the same type of service provided by different operators. In addition, the Agency specifies the quality parameters, the method of measurement and publication, the timeframes for the delivery of operator-conducted measurements, and the minimum service quality requirements.[90]

89. At the user's request, the operator may preserve records on the subscriber's academic or occupational title, as well as other data, for a fee, as long as this does not compromise the rights of third parties. The operator may use subscriber data exclusively for the purposes of registration, installation, conclusion, execution, amendment, or termination of the subscriber agreement, billing of services, and for the demands of qualified authorities, while for other purposes only with the explicit authorization of the subscriber whose data are processed. The operator is obligated to modify or withdraw the subscriber's data at any time upon request. The operator is required to retain subscriber data for a minimum of one year following the termination of service provision.[91]

90. Based on Article 181 of the LEC, the operator is obliged to retain particular data on traffic and location and relevant data required for identification and registration of subscribers, both legal and natural persons, to the extent to which such data were generated or processed by them, for the purposes of defense and national security, as well as crime prevention, investigation, detection, and criminal prosecution of crime offenders, assistance in search and rescue of people, and protection of human life, health, and property, in accordance with the law. The categories of data that should be retained, in accordance with the provisions of Article 182 of the LEC,

88. Article 36 of the Law on Electronic Communications of Montenegro.
89. Article 39 of the Law on Electronic Communications of Montenegro.
90. Article 155 of the Law on Electronic Communications of Montenegro.
91. Article 174 of the Law on Electronic Communications of Montenegro.

are determined in detail by the Rulebook on technical and organizational conditions for downloading retained data ("Official Gazette of Montenegro" No. 54/15) and the Regulation on the category of retained electronic communications data ("Official Gazette of Montenegro" No. 52/14).

Chapter 6. Regulation of Broadcasting Activities (Audiovisual Services)

91. Audiovisual services in Montenegro are primarily governed by the Law on Electronic Media (LEM).[92] The LEM governs the rights, obligations, and responsibilities of legal and natural persons engaged in the activity of producing and providing audiovisual media services (hereinafter: AVM services), electronic publication services via electronic communications networks of competencies, status, and funding sources in order to prevent unauthorized media concentration and promote media pluralism.

92. Article 46 of the LEM prescribes that AVM service may be in the form of:

(1) electronic media (radio or television broadcasting);
(2) on-demand AVM service;
(3) audiovisual commercial communication.[93]

93. In addition, the Law on Public Broadcasting Service (Official Gazette of Montenegro, Nos. 57/14 and 24/17) establishes the legal framework for the public service broadcaster in Montenegro, including the obligations, funding, governance, and programming requirements of the public broadcaster.

94. A general regulatory framework for media activities in Montenegro, including audiovisual services, is provided by the Law on Media (Official Gazette of Montenegro, Nos. 44/12 and 15/19), which covers various aspects such as media ownership, journalistic ethics, access to information, and the rights and responsibilities of media outlets.

95. The legislative authority for Montenegro's audiovisual policy is the Ministry of Culture and Media of Montenegro. The Agency for Electronic Media of Montenegro (AEM) is the main regulatory authority for AVM services in Montenegro with a separate legal entity, functionally independent of any state body and all legal and natural persons generating and broadcasting radio and television programs or providing other AVM services.[94]

96. On the scope of its responsibilities, the Agency is required to:

(1) provide the AVM Services Development Program;
(2) draft an overview for the development of a plan for the use of the radio-frequency band designated for terrestrial broadcasting in collaboration with the regulatory body responsible for electronic communications;

92. Law on Electronic Media of Montenegro (Official Gazette of Montenegro Nos. 046/10 of Aug. 6, 2010, 040/11 of Aug. 8, 2011, 053/11 of Nov. 11, 2011, 006/13 of Jan. 31, 2013, 055/16 of Aug. 17, 2016).
93. Article 46 of the Law on Electronic Media of Montenegro.
94. Agency for Electronic Media of Montenegro (AEM), https://www.rirm.org/, May 12, 2022.

(3) approve the draft plan for allocating radio frequencies for terrestrial broadcasting;
(4) advise the regulatory body for electronic communication on the necessity of designating an operator with SMP if the analysis determines that the relevant electronic communication services market, which is the basis for the provision of and/or access to AVM services, is not sufficiently competitive;
(5) issue licenses for AVM service provision (broadcasting license and on-demand AVM service provision license);
(6) establish the quantity of the fee for the issuance and use of an AVM service provision license;
(7) maintain a database of AVM service providers and electronic publications;
(8) resolve in accordance with the complaints of natural and legal persons concerning the operation of AVM service providers;
(9) supervise the implementation of the law;
(10) enact and enforce supplementary legislation.[95]

95. Article 12 of the Law on Electronic Media of Montenegro.

Chapter 7. Regulation of Online Interactive Services (Electronic Commerce, Online Platforms, B2B Platforms)

97. Online interactive services in Montenegro are regulated by the Electronic Commerce Law[96] (ECL) and the Law on Consumer Protection[97] (LCP).

98. ECL regulates the services normally provided for remuneration at a distance by means of electronic equipment for the processing and storage of data (hereinafter: information society services), liability of information society services' providers, and procedure regarding the contracts in electronic form. According to the ECL, information society services providers are required to register in the Central Register of Business Entities and to make their data accessible to the relevant government agencies.[98]

99. The ECL does not require a special permit, approval, or concession for providing information society service in Montenegro.[99] However, the state administration authority responsible for the information may take one or more measures to restrict the freedom to provide information society services to a service provider based in a Member State of the EU whose service poses a serious threat to the legal order, particularly regarding the execution of investigative actions, the identification and prosecution of criminal offenders, the protection of minors, and the fight against the incitement of hatred or intolerance based on race, gender, religion, or nationality, while also infringing upon personal dignity:

(1) Public health, life, and well-being of the citizens.
(2) Security and defense of Montenegro.
(3) Consumer protection, encompassing the interests of investors.[100]

100. Limitation measures may include:

(1) public announcement of possible illegal actions of providers of information society services;
(2) an order to the service provider to take measures to eliminate the identified irregularities;
(3) prohibition of certain actions;
(4) temporary suspension of computer operations, databases, and peripheral devices;
(5) temporary prohibition on conducting activities;
(6) criminal charge;

96. Electronic Commerce Law and (Official Gazette of Montenegro, No. 80/2004, Nos. 41/2010 and 56/2013).
97. Law on Consumer Protection (Official Gazette of Montenegro, Nos. 2/2014, 6/2014, 43/2015, 70/2017, 67/2019 and 146/2021).
98. Article 7 of the Electronic Commerce Law of Montenegro.
99. Article 6 of the Electronic Commerce Law of Montenegro.
100. Article 6a of the Electronic Commerce Law of Montenegro.

(7) an order to a legal entity that provides public services (the provision of electronic communications services, etc.) to suspend the provision of services to the service provider whose activities have been suspended.[101]

101. The state bodies in Montenegro are obliged to collaborate with the relevant authority of the EU Member State and the European Commission in the field of information society services for electronic exchange of:

(1) general information regarding contractual rights and obligations, complaints procedures, and other legal remedies;
(2) essential information related to the authorities, associations, and organizations responsible for providing additional information;
(3) data at the request of a Member State of the EU or the European Commission and the provision of assistance.[102]

102. Domestic courts are obliged to resolve disputes on lawsuits for the protection of rights in the field of the information society by urgent procedure.[103] Beside judicial protection, the ECL stipulates out-of-court settlement of disputes by providing a possibility for the user and information society services provider to arrange the resolution of mutual disputes by agreeing to an arbitration procedure/mediation in accordance with the law. The arbitrators or mediators are obliged to deliver the decisions to the competent authority in accordance with the law regulating the arbitration procedure/mediation.[104]

103. LCP provides a general framework for the protection of consumer rights by a comprehensive set of provisions to ensure fair and transparent transactions and safeguard consumer interests, such as the right to accurate information, the right to free choice, the right to product safety, the right to equitable contractual terms, the right to warranty, and the rights to redress and compensation. LCP covers specific provisions for distance contracts (concluded online, by telephone, or by mail) and off-premises contracts (concluded outside of business premises). It places responsibility on manufacturers, importers, and distributors to ensure the safety of products offered on the market and defines mechanisms for consumers to seek redress, including the possibility of mediation or initiating legal proceedings.

104. Article 64 stipulates that before concluding a distance contract, the vendor must provide the consumer with all of the key contract terms (prior notice obligation). In the situation of unauthorized use of a payment card with regard to a distance transaction, consumer has the right to request a refund of the paid amount.[105]

---

101. Article 6b of the Electronic Commerce Law of Montenegro.
102. Article 22a of the Electronic Commerce Law of Montenegro.
103. Article 22c of the Electronic Commerce Law of Montenegro.
104. Article 22d of the Electronic Commerce Law of Montenegro.
105. Article 72 of the Law on Consumer Protection of Montenegro.

In addition, LCP defines "unfair business practices" as aggressive commercial tactics if the vendor contacts the customer repeatedly and against his will via electronic means of communication.[106]

105. The consumer has the right to unilaterally withdraw from the distance contract within fourteen days from the moment of delivery of the product to the consumer or a third party specifically designated by the consumer. The consumer's right to withdraw from the distance contract is excluded in the following cases:

(1) the trader has completely executed the service contract, and execution has commenced with the consumer's prior explicit consent and confirmation that he is aware that he would be deprived of the right to withdraw from the contract;
(2) the subject of the contract is goods or services whose price is determined by changes in the financial market that are beyond the vendor's control and may occur during the duration of the consumer's right to unilaterally withdraw from the contract;
(3) the subject of the contract is goods made to the consumer's requirements or designed for the consumer;
(4) the subject of the contract is easily perishable goods;
(5) the subject of the contract is sealed items that, if opened after delivery, are not suitable for return owing to health or hygiene concerns;
(6) the contract's subject is goods that, by definition, are inseparably combined with other things after delivery;
(7) the subject of the contract is the delivery of alcoholic beverages, the price of which is agreed upon at the time of contract conclusion, and delivery may take place after thirty days if the price is affected by market movements beyond the vendor's control;
(8) the consumer specifically requested a visit from the trader to take out urgent repairs or maintenance unless, during such a visit, the trader also provided other services, i.e., delivered other goods that are not required for carrying out urgent repairs or maintenance work;
(9) the contract's subject is the delivery of sealed audio or video recordings, i.e., computer programs that were opened after delivery;
(10) the subject of the contract is the delivery of daily newspapers, journals, or magazines;
(11) a contract provided by a public tender;
(12) the subject of the contract for the provision of accommodation services that are not intended for housing, transportation of goods, vehicle rental services, food and beverage delivery services, or services related to leisure activities if the service is agreed to be provided on a specific date or within a specific time period;

106. Article 117 of the Law on Consumer Protection of Montenegro.

(13) the subject of the contract is the delivery of digital content that was not delivered on a permanent medium if the contract was started with the consumer's prior express consent and confirmation that he is aware that by consenting, he rejects his right to unilateral termination of the contract.[107]

107. Article 74j of the Law on Consumer Protection of Montenegro.

Chapter 8. Regulation of Cryptography and Dual-Use Goods

106. The dual-use goods in Montenegro are governed by the Law on Control of Export of Dual-Use Goods[108] (LCEDUG), which regulates the terms and conditions for the export and transit of dual-use goods, the provision of brokering services and technical assistance in relation to dual-use items, the powers and duties of state authorities, and other relevant concerns for dual-use item export and transit.

107. Dual-use goods, within the meaning of LCEDUG, are goods, including software and technology, that can be used for civilian and military purposes, namely:

(1) goods that can be used for the design, development, production, or use of nuclear, chemical, and biological weapons and means of their delivery, including goods that can be used for non-explosive purposes and that can help in the production of nuclear weapons or other nuclear explosive devices;
(2) cyber-surveillance technology that can be used to commit serious violations of human rights or international humanitarian law or that can pose a threat to international security or the security interests of Montenegro.[109]

108. Article 3 defines the export of dual-use goods as:

(1) sending or delivering goods from the territory of Montenegro in accordance with customs regulations;
(2) re-export of goods in accordance with customs regulations, except for goods in transit;
(3) passive processing procedures in accordance with customs regulations; or
(4) transfer of software or technology via electronic media, fax, telephone, e-mail, or other electronic means outside of Montenegro, which includes making available in electronic form that software and technology outside of Montenegro, i.e., by direct transfer of technology via electronic means of communication.[110]

109. Based on the proposal of the national authority in charge of international trade affairs, the Government of Montenegro authorizes the National Dual-Use Items Control List.[111] The verification of the end user certificate on the end use of the goods (End User Certificate, EUC) or the international import certificate (International Import Certificate, IIC) is performed by the state administration body

108. The Law on Control of Export of Dual-Use Goods in Montenegro ("Official Gazette of Montenegro," No. 145/21 dated 31.12.2021).
109. Article 2 of the Law on Control of Export of Dual-Use Goods in Montenegro.
110. Article 3 of the Law on Control of Export of Dual-Use Goods in Montenegro.
111. Article 5 of the Law on Control of Export of Dual-Use Goods in Montenegro.

responsible for foreign affairs. If dual-use goods are intended for placement on the market of Montenegro, the Ministry can issue an End User Certificate (EUC) or an International Import Certificate (IIC) if requested by the exporting country.[112]

112. Article 15 of the Law on Control of Export of Dual-Use Goods in Montenegro.

Part II. Online Public Services

110. The process of digital transformation of the Montenegrin PA and the introduction of e-services are key components of the process of PA Reform.[113] Digitalization of public services became a priority for the Government of Montenegro during the COVID-19 pandemic, which highlighted the necessity of faster overall digital development and, in particular, the significance of the availability of public services to citizens, businesses, and other public groups via the internet. The 42nd Government of Montenegro, after it was elected on December 4, 2020, initiated the assessment on the state of play of institutional capacities regarding e-government preparedness, especially within the Ministry of Public Administration (MPA), Digital Society and Media (MPADSM) as the critical carrier of this process, as well as all other public institutions committed to digitalization. The findings were translated into the Digital Transformation Strategy of Montenegro 2022–2026 with the Action Plan for 2022–2023, adopted by the Government of Montenegro on December 21, 2021.[114] This strategy constitutes the umbrella strategic document in the field of digitalization, which defines the prerequisites and initiatives needed for rapid adaptation to an increasingly complex digital environment and the agile and proactive development of digital Montenegro.[115]

113. Public Administration Reform Strategy 2022–2026 with the Action Plan for 2022–2024, Government of Montenegro (https://www.gov.me/dokumenta/823842f4-2ffd-4a0d-936e-c1b00c669115, accessed May 3, 2023).

114. Digital Transformation Strategy of Montenegro 2022–2026 with the Action Plan for 2022–2023, Government of Montenegro (https://www.gov.me/clanak/strategija-digitalne-transformacije-za-razvoj-digitalne-crne-gore, accessed May 3, 2023).

115. *Ibid.*

Chapter 1. e-Government Legal Framework

111. In a wider framework, digitalization of public services is recognized by the Law on Administrative Procedure (LAP), which regulates the rules that have to be observed, with a view to achieving protection of the rights and legal interests of individuals, legal entities, or other parties, as well as to protection of the public interest, by the state authorities, state administration bodies, local self-government bodies, local government bodies, institutions and other entities exercising public powers when they, while directly applying the regulations, decide and perform other administrative activities in administrative matters.[116] However, there are inconsistencies in the terminology used in LAP and the key laws regulating e-Government due to the fact that LAP precedes these laws. It is necessary to amend LAP in order to harmonize the terminology referring to e-Government services with the relevant laws so as to avoid inconsistencies and ambiguities leading to arbitrary interpretation of certain provisions by public law authorities or parties in administrative proceedings.

112. The core legal framework regulating the field of e-Government consists of the Law on Electronic Government (LEG), the Law on Electronic Identification and Electronic Signature (LEIES), the Law on Information Security (LIS), the Law on Electronic Documents (LED) and the Law on Electronic Commerce (LEC).[117] However, it is important to also mention the Law on Administrative Fees (LAF) as part of the e-Government legal framework, given that submission of proof of paid administrative fees, which can also be electronic, is requested in applications for administrative procedures.[118]

113. The LEG was adopted by the Parliament of Montenegro in December 2019, but its implementation started in July 2021 amidst the COVID-19 pandemic. In contrast to the previously valid LEG, the current one lays down more extensively and accurately the manner of functioning of electronic government, as well as the rights and obligations of PA institutions when using e-Government. Subject of LEG are state authorities, state administration authorities, state agencies, state funds, and other holders of public authority, including local self-government bodies, local government bodies, special and public services within the meaning of the law regulating local self-government, independent and regulatory bodies, and legal and natural persons exercising public powers.[119]

114. As prescribed by Article 3 of LEG, e-Government functions through the authorities' single information system, authorities' information and communication

116. Article 1, Law on Administrative Procedure ("Official Gazette of Montenegro" Nos. 056/14, 020/15, 040/16, 037/17).
117. Article 6, Law on Electronic Government ("Official Gazette of Montenegro" No. 072/19).
118. Article 11, Law on Administrative Fees (Official Gazette of Montenegro No. 018/19).
119. Articles 1 and 2, Law on Electronic Government ("Official Gazette of Montenegro" No. 072/19).

network, and the system for electronic data exchange, as well as through information systems established by the authorities and other subjects. In Article 8, paragraph 1, item 1, *e-Government service* is defined as the proceeding of authorities and other entities towards the user, another authority, or another entity when receiving, exchanging, processing, delivering, or publishing data, submissions, acts, and other documents or other forms of communication within the scope of their competence, using ICT. The same article defines in item 10 *submission in electronic form* as a request, proposal, application, request, appeal, petition, complaint, and other submission by which a party addresses an authority or other entity in electronic form, whereas in item 11 states that an *act in electronic form* is any document that initiates, supplements, changes, ceases or terminates an official action of an authority or other entity in electronic form.

115. A key component of the e-Government infrastructure, functioning of which is in detail prescribed in LEG, is the Meta-Register, a single record of all electronic registers and information management systems in the PA managed by MPADSM. In case of changes (modifications, deletions, or additions) of data on the electronic register, that is, the information system, the respective authority, or other entity is obliged to submit to MPADSM data on the change in the prescribed form within ten days from the date of the change.[120]

116. LEG prescribes in Article 27 that each authority, or other entity, is obliged to prepare and publish on its website up-to-date records of the e-services it provides, which contain the conditions for providing the e-service, the method of entering submissions, and the delivery of documents in electronic form, as well as the method of payment of administrative fees from Article 28 of this law and, at the same time, submit it to MPADSM in electronic form. While there are no legal obstacles to the digitalization of PA services, it is paramount that authorities and other relevant entities ensure the technical conditions for the sound implementation of LEG.

117. LEIES was adopted by the Parliament of Montenegro in April 2017 and entered into force in May 2017. This law regulates the conditions for the use of electronic signatures, electronic seals, electronic time stamps, and electronic registered delivery services in legal transactions, administrative, judicial, and other proceedings and certification for website authentication, as well as the electronic identification system and requirements for the recognition of other states' electronic identification means.[121]

120. Article 23, *ibid.*

121. Article 1, Law on Electronic Identification and Electronic Signature ("Official Gazette of Montenegro" Nos. 031/17, 072/19).

118. Three types of electronic signatures are recognized by LEIES, i.e., (1) *electronic signature*, (2) *advanced electronic signature,* and (3) *qualified electronic signature.*[122] The main difference between these three types of signatures is the level of security they provide to both the signatory and the recipient of the signed act, as well as the issuing modality.

119. Article 12 of LEIES stipulates that the validity and admissibility of an electronic signature cannot be disputed only because: (1) it is in electronic form; or (2) it is not based on a qualified electronic signature certificate. The legal effect of electronic signature and advanced electronic signature is reinforced by Article 13, which states that the authority or legal entity cannot refuse to receive an electronic document with an electronic signature or an advanced electronic signature just because it is in electronic form. Furthermore, Article 14 equalizes the qualified electronic signature with the handwritten signature by stipulating that the qualified electronic signature has the same legal effect as a handwritten signature, i.e., a handwritten signature and seal in relation to data in paper form and is admissible as evidence in proceedings before state authorities, state administration authorities, local self-government authorities and local administration authorities and legal entities that perform public powers.

120. In contrast to the EU electronic IDentification, Authentication and trust Services (eIDAS) Regulation, which in Article 25 stipulates that an *electronic signature* shall not be denied *legal effect* and admissibility as *evidence in legal proceedings* solely on the grounds that it is in an electronic form or that it does not meet the requirements for qualified electronic signatures, LEIES specifies this legal effect in legal proceedings only for the qualified electronic signature (*see above*), and not for the electronic signature and advanced electronic signature. Hereby, it is important that regulations regulating specific e-services clearly define the type of signature that is required for signing a specific act.

121. The Parliament of Montenegro adopted the LED in November 2022, and it entered into force in December 2022. LED brings significantly improved solutions over the applicable law. This law regulates the use of electronic documents in legal transactions, administrative, judicial, and other proceedings, as well as the rights, obligations, and responsibilities of business companies, entrepreneurs, independent and regulatory bodies, and other legal and natural persons, state authorities, state administration authorities, state agencies, state funds and other holders of public authority, local self-government authorities, local government authorities, special and public services in terms of the law governing local self-government if the law does not specify otherwise.[123]

122. LED defines an *electronic document* as a set of data that is electronically formatted or stored on an electronic, magnetic, optical, or other medium and that contains properties that identify the creator, establish the credibility of the content,

122. Articles 9, 10 and 11, *ibid.*
123. Article 1, Law on Electronic Document ("Official Gazette of Montenegro" No. 132/2022).

and prove the immutability of the content over time, and include all forms of written text, data, images, drawings, maps, sound, music, speech, as well as digitized documents, and the like.

123. Pursuant to Article 5 of LED, an electronic document has the same legal validity as a document made on paper, and its validity and probative value cannot be disputed just because it is in electronic form if its use and circulation are carried out in accordance with this law. This means that an electronic document compliant with this law has the same legal effect in legal proceedings and transactions as a paper document.

124. In terms of the structure, LED prescribes in Article 8 that an electronic document necessarily consists of two inseparable parts: (1) a general part, which makes up the content of the document; and (2) a separate part, consisting of one or more embedded electronic signatures, i.e., seals, data on the time of creation (completion of creation) of the electronic document, as well as other documentation features and other structured records. There are no specifications regarding the type of electronic signature that an electronic document can be signed by.

125. Article 10 of LED stipulates that an electronic document originally created in electronic form and signed with an electronic signature, i.e., an electronic seal, is considered the original and that an electronic document cannot have a copy in electronic form. If the same person creates two documents with the same content, in electronic form and on paper, those documents are considered independent.

126. In Article 11, it is prescribed that a copy of the electronic document on paper is made by printing the external form of the appearance of the electronic document on paper. Certification of a copy of an electronic document on paper is carried out in accordance with the law governing the certification of signatures, handwriting, and transcripts. Certification of a copy of an electronic document on paper can also be performed by the competent authorities when a certified copy is required in the proceedings conducted before those authorities.

127. LED defines a digitized document as a copy of a document that was not originally created in electronic form. A digitized document has the same legal validity as a document that was not originally created in electronic form, if the following conditions are met, i.e., (1) the digitization was performed under the supervision of a person authorized to certify signatures, manuscripts, and transcripts, in accordance with the law regulating the certification of signatures, manuscripts, and transcripts, or an authorized person of the competent authority; (2) the identity of the digitized document with the document that was not originally created in electronic form is confirmed by a qualified electronic seal or a qualified electronic signature of the person referred to in point (1); and (3) contains a mark that it is a digitally certified copy.[124] Amendments to the Law on Certification of Signatures, Manuscripts,

124. Article 15, *ibid.*

and Transcripts were adopted by the Parliament of Montenegro in December 2022 in order to enable such certification and to prescribe the conditions for the certification of these documents.

128. In the legal framework of e-Government, it is important to also consider the LAF, given that pursuant to Article 11, which defines the manner of fees payment, the taxpayer is obliged to submit the appropriate proof of the paid fee, which can also be electronic. Furthermore, it stipulates that in the case of electronic fee payment, the fee is paid through the system for electronic collection of administrative fees, which is managed by the state administration authority responsible for e-Government and e-Business.

129. Decree on detailed conditions and manner of paying administrative fees electronically[125] in Article 2 paragraph 2 prescribes that payment is made: (1) using payment cards at the counters of the competent state administration authorities, local self-government units, and legal entities exercising public authority; and (2) through the electronic services portal. Electronic payment of administrative fees is an essential element in the process of digitalization of public services and overall digital transformation.

130. For LEC, *see* above Part I, Chapter 7, and for LIS, *see* below Part V.

125. Decree on detailed conditions and manner of paying administrative fees electronically ("Official Gazette of Montenegro" 068/20).

Chapter 2. Legal Framework for e-Health

131. Reforms in the healthcare system in Montenegro are followed by the development of an integral health information system with the aim of supporting new payment methods (business information system) and medical processes at all levels of healthcare (medical information system). The integral system included the development of IT support for the Health Insurance Fund (HIF), the health-statistical information system of the Institute for Public Health to support reporting, the system of the Institute for Medicines and Medical Devices, and the Ministry of Health.

132. The legal framework regulating eHealth services is based primarily on the core legal framework of e-Government (*see* above) and more specifically defined by the Law on Health Protection (LHP)[126] and a set of specific bylaws. It is important to mention the Rulebook on the detailed content and method of keeping basic medical documentation, which entered into force in February 2022 and, for the first time, defines the legal regulation and content of the Electronic Health Record.

133. LHP prescribes in Article 61a that for the purpose of systematic monitoring of the development of healthcare and provision of healthcare, the Ministry of Health keeps records of issued decisions to health institutions that meet the conditions for performing healthcare activities in *electronic form*. The records from paragraph 1 of this article are regularly updated and published by the Ministry on its website. The processing, exchange, and publication of data from paragraph 1 of this article in electronic form are carried out in accordance with the laws regulating electronic administration, electronic identification and electronic signature, electronic document, electronic commerce, and information security.

134. Article 136 of the LHP stipulates in paragraphs 1 and 3 that the medical documentation that is created during the provision of healthcare by public healthcare institutions, as well as the documentation that is created during the provision of healthcare by other entities that provide healthcare or is created during the provision of healthcare outside of Montenegro, should be kept in paper or *electronic form*. Furthermore, paragraph 2 prescribes that when providing healthcare directly, the healthcare worker is obliged to sign the medical documentation by hand and certify it with a facsimile or sign it with an electronic signature in accordance with the law.

135. Pursuant to the Statute of the HIF Article 7, paragraphs 17, 19, and 20, within the framework of its competences: (i) keeps records of all data related to the implementation and realization of healthcare and health insurance within the integral health information system; (ii) ensures the functioning of the integral health information system and participates in providing support for its definition and implementation; (iii) enables electronic exchange of data between providers of

126. Law on Health Protection ("Official Gazette of Montenegro," Nos. 3/2016, 39/2016, 2/2017, 44/2018, 24/2019—other laws, 82/2020 and 8/2021).

health services and managers of data collections, develops and maintains information and communication infrastructure and ensures protection and storage of data.[127]

136. Online health services are available to citizens and users of health insurance via the web address (www.ezdravlje.me) or the corresponding mobile application (eZdravlje.me). The eHealth portal enables the use and provision of information about electronic services in the health system of Montenegro. Registration is done by entering the health card number (a ten-digit number written on the first page of the health card) or the number of the new ID card and PIN code. In order to be able to access electronic services, it is necessary for citizens to contact the competent regional unit/branch of the HIF or send a request electronically to the portal in order to obtain the appropriate PIN code. With the PIN code, each insured person receives basic information on how to access the Portal. For an insured person who is a minor, i.e., an insured person deprived of legal capacity, the PIN code can be taken over by his legal representative or guardian (parent, guardian, etc.). Insured persons who did not select a doctor do not have the option of using the services provided by the selected doctor (e-Schedule and e-Ordering).

137. The e-Health system offers a set of services for citizens. e-Scheduling is a service for online scheduling of visits with selected doctors in health centers (selected doctor for adults, selected doctor for women, and selected doctor for children). e-Scheduling allows online scheduling of visits, as well as checking, canceling, or changing appointments. In this way, all types of visits can be scheduled, except for preventive examinations (consultations for children and regular immunizations) and home visits by selected doctors. Service may be used by insured persons of the HIF who are registered with selected doctors in Health Centers.

138. e-Prescription is an electronic service that enables patients to view prescribed and realized prescriptions online using advanced technologies and devices (PC, Smartphone, Tablet devices, etc.). Patients can receive information on their account at any time about prescriptions that are prescribed and ongoing, as well as prescriptions that have been implemented in the last six months with information on where and when they were implemented. In this way, the availability of information to citizens, i.e., to insured persons in the domain of healthcare, is improved, considering that in the healthcare system in Montenegro, the printed version of the prescription is no longer in use (except in specific cases).

139. e-Result is an electronic service that enables patients to view the results of biochemical laboratory analyses online, with the use of appropriate applications and newer-generation devices. The service was developed for the needs of insured persons, with the aim of making information about the services provided (analyses) and the results of laboratory findings available to patients as soon as possible. In this way, patients can chronologically follow and search the results of biochemical

127. Statute of the Health Insurance Fund of Montenegro ("Official Gazette of Montenegro," No. 021/20).

analyses performed at the health center. This service is available to citizens thanks to the successful implementation of the laboratory information system project in health centers in Montenegro, which have centers for laboratory diagnostics in their composition. The activities of introducing the laboratory information system are ongoing in other public health institutions in Montenegro (e.g., general hospitals).

140. e-Pharmacy is an electronic service intended for citizens (patients), developed with the aim of providing information on the availability of medicines in all pharmacies in the territory of Montenegro, which have signed contracts with HIF for the supply of medicines to insured persons. Through the portal and mobile application, insured persons receive precise information about which pharmacies they can take the prescribed therapy. This service has its application and great importance in case of possible changes in the availability of certain medicines, more precisely in case of deficiencies or shortages of certain medicines.

141. e-Insurance is an electronic service that enables citizens (insured persons) to view the status of their health insurance as a basis for exercising rights from health care in health institutions in Montenegro at the expense of the funds of HIF. In addition to this, citizens (insured persons) also have information about their obligation to pay contributions. Data available to patients are automatically downloaded through electronic exchange from the registers of competent institutions (Tax Administration and Ministry of the Interior).

142. e-Ordering is an electronic service intended for insured persons of the Fund who are registered with selected doctors in health centers. This service enables electronic ordering of prescriptions (therapy) for chronic patients, remittances, and confirmations.

143. e-ExerciseofRights is an electronic service designed in such a way as to provide all insured persons of the HIF with an overview of the documents on the exercised right from health insurance.

144. COVID-19 is an electronic service developed during the COVID-19 pandemic, intended for insured persons tested for the presence of the new coronavirus and for the purpose of receiving feedback on the test results.

145. e-EK is an electronic service that allows insured persons to view the costs of exercising their health insurance rights (which are primarily exercised in HIF), the costs of exercising the right to health care (which is exercised in public and private health institutions), as well as the costs of exercising other rights, for which there are electronic records in the Integral Information System of Health (IISZ). In this way, the insured person can inspect the amounts of part of the funds from the mandatory health insurance, i.e., the funds of HIF used to exercise their rights. This does not include all the financial resources that HIF allocates for the stated purposes, and due to the complex way of financing health care in some specific segments, which are not paid or reported per insured person but in a fixed amount, based on the value of the team that provides services, the value of program activities, etc.

146. The SafeGO CG service enables the issuance of an EU digital COVID certificate. The EU digital COVID certificate contains a QR code, which is digitally signed to protect against misuse.

Chapter 3. Online Voting

147. The basis of the electoral system is laid out in the Constitution of Montenegro and later elaborated by specific laws and bylaws, which govern elections. The electoral legislation consists of the following key laws:

- Law on the Election of Councilors and Members of Parliament.
- Law on the Electoral Register.
- Law on the Election of the President of Montenegro.
- Law on Political Parties.
- Law on Financing of Political Entities and Election Campaigns.

148. None of these laws stipulates the possibility of online voting.

Chapter 4. Other e-Government Services

149. The umbrella web address providing access to all e-Government services is www.euprava.me.[128] The portal is an access point to various information and public services, which are under the jurisdiction of state authorities, as well as links to local self-government authorities and public bodies, and its main purpose is to provide online communication between citizens and legal entities with the state administration, as well as within the state administration.

150. According to the level of access, information is classified into information of general public interest, including information about electronic services, which can be available to everyone, and protected information, which can only be accessed by registered users. Information and e-services on the Portal are grouped in several ways so that users can easily access the desired services. Information is grouped according to life situations so that they follow all important situations for individuals (education, business, issuing of documents, etc.) or legal entities (business and work, documents, finances, etc.), as well as for PA.[129]

151. The portal supports the following categories of users: (i) *Anonymous users*—users who access the Portal anonymously, without prior registration; (ii) *Users registered by email*—users who access the Portal by registering with an email address, without using qualified and valid certificates; (iii) *Registered users*—users who log in to the Portal using qualified and valid digital certificates. The Portal enables (i) anonymous users to use e-services at the level of information on procedures, contact information for the implementation of procedures, and other necessary information on institutions, as well as all information of public importance that has the character of free access. These users access the Portal as any information website and use it at that level. The Portal enables (ii) users registered by e-mail to use the e-services, in addition to receiving information, at the level of submitting requests for services that do not require a digital signature; and (iii) registered users can be individuals, legal entities, and PA employees who use the services of the Portal, as well as authorized officials of competent institutions (PA employees) in charge of creating services and providing services on the eGovernment portal.[130]

152. Registered users can use the services of the Portal at the highest level that has been implemented; for example, individuals and businesses can, for certain services, obtain the form (request) necessary to obtain the service, fill it in, sign it electronically, pay the administrative fee electronically and send the request electronically. The portal assigns each request to the competent institution, where it is processed in a traditional manner or electronically. The registered user can check the status of his/her request at any time. This procedure applies to both individuals and legal entities. Registered users employed in institutions responsible for public services have been assigned appropriate rights recognized by the Portal, and

128. eGovernment Portal, Government of Montenegro (www.euprava.me, accessed May 20, 2023).
129. *Ibid.*
130. *Ibid.*

depending on this, they can set up an e-service, create electronic forms on the Portal, monitor user requests, administer electronic public discussion on the Portal, etc. The portal stores the history of all activities and the identities of all participants in the process.

153. A significant e-service which should be singled out is the social e-Card or Social Care Information System (SCIS). This service forms the backbone of the reform of the social and child protection system with the aim of providing socially vulnerable categories with the highest possible quality social protection, both in terms of material benefits and in terms of social and child protection services. The implementation of SCIS required a reform of the legal and institutional framework—the drafting of the new Law on Social and Child Protection and key bylaws, which was initiated and still undergoing; introduction of standards, reorganization and expansion of the network of centers for social work, creation of new job descriptions, systematization and most importantly re-engineering of procedures/business processes in centers for social work, as well as unified procedures.

154. In terms of public access to information in line with the Law on Free Access to Information (LFAI),[131] Montenegro renewed its membership in the initiative Open Government Partnership (OGP)[132] by adopting the National Action Plan (NAP) for 2018–2020 for the implementation of this initiative. The web-portal https://www.otvorenauprava.me offers the interested public access to information on current developments of the initiative and implementation of the Action Plan. The NAP 2018–2020 included five obligations:

- improvement of public services;
- participation of citizens;
- increasing public integrity;
- more efficient management of public resources;
- access to information.

155. In 2021, the process of co-creating a new NAP began. After the end of the implementation period of the NAP 2018–2020, MPADSM initiated the process of preparing a new NAP, with a special focus on the areas of transparency and accountability of PA, innovation, digitization, the fight against corruption, and participatory democracy. In 2022, the process of forming a new Operational Team for the OGP in Montenegro began, which is still ongoing.

156. LFAI, OGP, and Directive 2013/37/EU amending Directive 2003/98/EC on the re-use of public sector information, which emphasizes the need to publish datasets in a machine-readable and open format together with metadata, provide the legal basis for the open data portal www.data.gov.me. The portal is a place where

131. Law on Free Access to Information ("Official Gazette of Montenegro," Nos. 44/2012 and 30/2017).
132. Open Government Partnership (www.otvorenauprava.me, accessed May 20, 2023).

PA authorities have the opportunity to publish data in an open format, within their jurisdiction, respecting the basic principles of publishing data for reuse. This portal is a central point for accessing public sector data, as well as a place of interaction with data users, business sector, IT and academic community, citizens, and other interested parties.[133]

157. Open data does not contain personal data or other data protected by law. This means that the principle of openness also includes the right of public authorities to retain certain data and thereby justify the trust of citizens, who must be sure that their right to privacy is protected in the process of data disclosure.[134]

158. The portal contains the following types of data:[135]

- Geo-spatial data—postal codes, national and local maps (cadastral maps and plans, topographic maps, maritime charts, and administrative boundaries help create maps that take into account surrounding buildings and roads).
- Cultural data—data on cultural works and artifacts. They provide an overview of the cultural assets and heritage of a country. They are most often owned by galleries, libraries, museums, and archives.
- Scientific data—data created as a result of conducted scientific research of all categories.
- Financial data—data such as government accounts (expenses and revenues) and information on financial markets (stocks, bills, etc.).
- Statistical data—national, regional, and local statistical data with main demographic and economic indicators (GDP, age, health, unemployment, income, education).
- Environment—hydrometeorological data, soil and water quality, energy consumption, emission levels.
- Traffic data—timetables of public transport (all types of transport) at the national, regional, and local levels, as well as information on road works, etc.
- Data on companies—registers of companies (lists of companies, ownership and management structure data, identification marks of registration, balance sheets).

133. Open Data Portal (www.data.gov.me, accessed May 20, 2023).
134. Government of Montenegro (https://www.gov.me/clanak/otvoreni-podaci-open-data, accessed May 20, 2023).
135. *Ibid.*

Part III. Online Transactions

Chapter 1. Electronic Contracting (Incl. Smart Contracts and Blockchain)

159. Pursuant to the Law on Electronic Commerce ("Official Gazette of the Republic of Montenegro," No. 080/04 dated December 29, 2004, Official Gazette of Montenegro," Nos. 041/10 dated July 23, 2010, 040/11 dated August 8, 2011, 056/ 13 of December 6, 2013), Article 10, the contract can be concluded electronically, i.e., in electronic form. The offer and acceptance of the offer can be made electronically, i.e., in electronic form. When an electronic message, i.e., electronic form, is used when concluding the contract, the validity of such a contract cannot be challenged just because it is in electronic form. The contract in electronic form is considered concluded the moment the offeror receives an electronic message containing the offeree's declaration of acceptance of the offer. The offer and acceptance of the offer, as well as other declarations of will made electronically, are considered received when the person to whom they are addressed can access them (Article 17).

160. Pursuant to the Law on Electronic Documents ("Official Gazette of Montenegro," No. 132/22 of December 5, 2022), an electronic document is a set of data that is electronically formatted or stored on an electronic, magnetic, optical, or other medium and that contains properties by which the creator is identified, the credibility of the content is determined and the immutability of the content is proven over time, and it includes all forms of written text, data, images, drawings, maps, sound, music, speech, as well as digitized documents and the like. An electronic document necessarily consists of two inseparable parts: (1) the general part, which constitutes the content of the document; and (2) a special part, consisting of one or more embedded electronic signatures, i.e., electronic seals, data on the time of creation (completion) of the electronic document, as well as other documentation properties and other structured records.

161. The development of digital currencies and blockchain technology in Montenegro is still in its infancy. Nevertheless, there is a tendency to make positive developments in this segment. The Central Bank of Montenegro has agreed to cooperate with the provider of crypto and blockchain solutions, the company "Ripple," in order to develop a strategy and implement a pilot program for the launch of the first digital currency in the country—the digital currency of the central bank (CBDC) or national stablecoin, i.e., stable currency. The introduction of digital currency is, in accordance with the basic goals of the Central Bank of Montenegro, another step forward toward the digitization of financial services and the expansion of the space for the availability of financial services to the citizens of Montenegro.

162. CBDC is a digitized version of currency issued by central banks. Today, over a hundred countries around the world are testing and developing a central bank digital currency for a wide range of needs, including strengthening financial inclusion, modernizing monetary policy, improving payment security, and increasing the efficiency of cross-border payments.

163. On April 11, 2023, the Governor of the Central Bank pointed out, "The Central Bank of Montenegro will work with the Government of Montenegro and the Montenegrin academic community to create a practical digital currency or a secure currency solution in order to test the main functionalities and potentials of blockchain technology, as well as to analyze the advantages and the risks that a CBDC or a national stablecoin could pose in terms of the availability of electronic means of payment, security, efficiency, regulatory compliance and most importantly the protection of the rights and privacy of end users."

164. Perper will be the first stablecoin in the world to use the latest and most revolutionary technology within the blockchain that enables instant payments. This is extremely important since the biggest problem with cryptocurrency payments is the time it takes for the funds to go from the payer to the biller.

165. Activities on the development of stablecoins are becoming more intense around the world; however, part of the public is still not familiar with this concept in detail, considering that most cryptocurrencies of this type are still in the development phase. It is a digital currency whose value is fixed to the value of an existing physical currency, which is why it is not characterized by price variations, as is the case with volatile cryptocurrencies, such as, for example, bitcoin.

166. At the same time, the European Central Bank is working on the development of the digital euro concept as a future means of safe, secure, and practical electronic payment in the eurozone.

167. For now, in Montenegro, there are no legal obstacles for any individual to buy or sell crypto-assets, but this also means that the risk he takes on himself is proportionately high. Regulation and supervision are the only ways to ensure the necessary trust: protecting end users, strengthening financial stability, and creating adequate conditions for the development of new digital banking services and payment instruments.

168. Considering the intensive work towards the development of blockchain technology, it can be said that there is no longer a need to implement contactless payment technology because at this stage it is pointless to buy existing licenses and recycled solutions from those markets that are themselves switching to blockchain, when possible directly focus on that technology.

169. The Government of Montenegro has repeatedly said that they are working on creating the text of the Law on the Regulation of Cryptocurrencies and Blockchain Technology and expressed their belief that in the future, it can be one of the new pillars of the Montenegrin economy. Digital money could be an extremely big advantage in the tourism sector, especially in those segments where Montenegro wants high-paying guests.

170. The position of the CBCG is that the draft law on blockchain technology and crypto-assets of the Ministry of Finance and Social Welfare of the Government in the previous term should follow EU regulations, especially the Regulation of the European Parliament and the Council on crypto-asset markets, i.e., the EU Markets in Crypto-Assets Act (MICA). Also, the CBCG insists on the transposition of the 6AMLD Directive, which regulates this issue from the point of view of money laundering and terrorist financing. Also, the IMF, the BIS, the Council of Europe, and the World Bank are logical choices of institutions whose advice and suggestions are of great importance in creating a legal framework based on the solution of the best comparative practices, which would ensure that we understand all the ways in which we can use the opportunities of crypto-assets and remove the new risks they bring. In that direction, the Ministry of Finance, the IMF, and the Council of Europe have already given their comments on the existing bill, and the CBCG will insist on their adoption.[136]

136. https://me.ekapija.com/news/3705258/crna-gora-i-kriptovalute-zakon-u-pripremi-cbcg-upozorava-na-spekulativna-obiljezja, May 31, 2023.

Chapter 2. Electronic Signatures

171. In Montenegro, the conditions for the application of the electronic signature have been met. Pursuant to the Law on Electronic Identification and Electronic Signature ("Official Gazette of Montenegro," No. 031/17 of May 12, 2017, 072/19 of December 26, 2019), an electronic signature is a set of data in electronic form that are attached or are logically connected to the electronic document and serve for the signature and electronic identification of the signatory. An electronic signature is created using a tool for creating an electronic signature and is based on a certificate for creating an electronic signature.

172. An advanced electronic signature is an electronic signature that reliably guarantees the identity of the signatory and the integrity of the electronic document and meets the conditions prescribed by the LEIES.

173. An advanced electronic signature must:

(1) be exclusively associated with the signatory;
(2) unambiguously identifies the signatory;
(3) is created by using means for creating an electronic signature that the signatory can manage independently and which is exclusively under his supervision;
(4) contains a direct connection with the data to which it refers in a way that unequivocally enables insight into any modification of the source data.

174. An advanced electronic signature based on an electronic certificate issued in a Member State of the EU is recognized as an advanced electronic signature in Montenegro if the aforementioned conditions are met.

175. A qualified electronic signature is an advanced electronic signature that is created using a qualified electronic signature tool and is based on a qualified electronic signature certificate.

176. The validity and admissibility of an electronic signature cannot be disputed only because:

(1) is in electronic form;
(2) is not based on a qualified electronic signature certificate.

177. The authority or legal entity cannot refuse to receive an electronic document with an electronic signature or an advanced electronic signature just because it is in electronic form.

178. A qualified electronic signature has the same legal effect as a handwritten signature, i.e., a handwritten signature and seal in relation to data in paper form, and is acceptable as a means of evidence in proceedings before state bodies, state administration bodies, local self-government bodies and local administration bodies and legal entities that perform public powers.

179. The existing legal framework on electronic identification and electronic census represents a valid basis for improving the process of digital transformation in Montenegro.

Chapter 3. Trust Services (Certificates, Electronic Mail Services, Etc.)

180. On the basis of Article 40 of the Law on Electronic Identification and Electronic Signature ("Official Gazette of Montenegro," Nos. 31/2017 and 72/2019) and the Rulebook on the detailed content and manner of keeping records of providers of electronic trust services and the register of qualified providers of electronic trust services ("Official Gazette of Montenegro," No. 20/2020) the MPA published the register of qualified providers of electronic trust services, namely: Pošta Crne Gore (Post of Montenegro), Coreit DOO Podgorica, Ministry of Internal Affairs, Crnogorski Telekom AD Podgorica, MPA, Post of Montenegro AD Podgorica, Coreit DOO Podgorica and Crnogorski Telekom AD Podgorica:

(1) Pošta Crne Gore AD Podgorica provides electronic trust services: Creation of a qualified certificate for an electronic signature, Creation of a qualified certificate for an electronic seal, Creation of a qualified time stamp, Creation of a qualified certificate for an internet page authentication and Qualified electronic registered delivery service.
(2) Coreit DOO Podgorica provides electronic trust services, namely: Creation of a qualified certificate for an electronic signature, Creation of a qualified certificate for an electronic seal, and Creation of a qualified time stamp.
(3) The Ministry of Internal Affairs is a qualified provider of electronic trust services, namely: Creation of a qualified certificate for a qualified electronic signature.
(4) Crnogorski Telekom AD Podgorica is a qualified provider of electronic trust services: Production of a qualified certificate for an advanced electronic seal, Production of a qualified certificate for an advanced electronic signature, Production of a qualified electronic time stamp, Production of a qualified certificate for a qualified electronic seal, Production of a qualified certificate for a qualified electronic signature, Qualified service of verification of qualified electronic signature and qualified electronic seal and Qualified service of electronic registered delivery.
(5) On the basis of Article 21 of the Law on Electronic Identification and Electronic Signature ("Official Gazette of Montenegro," Nos. 31/2017 and 72/2019) and the Rulebook on the manner of assessing the conformity of qualified means for the production of electronic signatures and electronic seals and the content of the list of certified qualified means for making electronic signatures and electronic seals ("Official Gazette of Montenegro," No. 20/2020) the MPA has published a list of certified qualified means for making electronic signatures and electronic seals, namely:
    (a) Gemalto, SafeNet eToken 5110, CC (comom criteria)—Pošta Crne Gore AD Podgorica.
    (b) Carte IAS Classic en version 4.4.2 avec serveur MOC 1.1 sur plateforme Multiapp v4.0.1; (IDPrime 940)—Coreit DOO Podgorica.
    (c) NXP Semiconductors; Model: ChipDoc P60 on JCOP 3 SECID P60 (OSB) SSCD; Verzija:v7b4—Ministry of Internal Affairs.

(d) Thales Group, SafeNet eToken 5110CC (940); Smart Card Platform: IDPrime MD940—Pošta Crne Gore AD Podgorica.
(e) Utimaco IS GmbH Model: CryptoServer CP5 Se500 Verzija: 5.1.0.0—Crnogorski Telekom AD Podgorica.

181. Based on Article 60b of the Law on Electronic Identification and Electronic Signature ("Official Gazette of Montenegro," Nos. 31/2017 and 72/2019), the MPA published the Register of Electronic Identification Systems, which includes two systems: (1) Certificate for electronic identification is issued on the identity card, which, in addition to this certificate, also contains a certificate for a qualified electronic signature (the authority that manages this electronic identification system is the Ministry of Internal Affairs with a high degree of security); (2) Ctrust eID system, established by Crnogorski Telekom. It is a means of electronic identification issued by Crnogorski Telekom based on the use of two authentication factors for connection with the user's identification data, namely one authentication factor based on knowledge, i.e., username/password—user name/password, and another authentication factor based on ownership, i.e., dynamic authentication factor—One Time Password (OTP), which is obtained through the eTrust authenticator mobile application. This system has a significant degree of security, although a shade lower than the previous one.

182. Services of creating certificates for electronic signatures and qualified certificates for electronic signatures, certificates for electronic seals and qualified certificates for electronic seals, certificates for authentication of websites and qualified certificates for authentication of websites, creation of electronic time stamps and qualified electronic time stamps, as well as services electronic registered delivery and qualified electronic registered delivery, verification of electronic signatures and electronic seals and qualified electronic signatures and qualified electronic seals and storage of electronic signatures and electronic seals or certificates related to those services and storage of qualified electronic signatures and qualified electronic seals or certificates that refer to these services (hereinafter: electronic trust services and qualified electronic trust services) for state administration bodies are performed in the manner prescribed by this rulebook on the manner of performing electronic trust services and qualified electronic trust services for state administration authorities ("Official Gazette of Montenegro Above," No. 020/20 of March 20, 2020).

Chapter 4. Online Financial Services

183. In the financial services sector, the dominant role is played by banks (90% of the total assets of the financial system), through which most of the financial business takes place. The second most important are insurance companies, dominated by those dealing with non-life insurance. The rest of the financial sector consists of microcredit financial institutions, investment funds, and leasing companies. Online shopping is constantly on the rise.

184. The bank offers financial services on a large scale through applications, and transactions can be monitored and executed via a mobile device from any location. In terms of online financial services, one of the major limitations of the Montenegrin economy is the impossibility of charging for services through the PayPal system. Despite the fact that this system has been present in Montenegro for several years, it is still possible to only make payments abroad but not to receive money through this payment system.

Chapter 5. Law of Evidence in the Digital Environment (Incl. Rules Regarding Electronic Archiving)

185. The Rulebook on the manner of management and functioning of the information system for document management ("Official Gazette of Montenegro," No. 062/15 of November 2, 2015) prescribes the manner of management and functioning of the information system for document management (hereinafter: information system eDMS) when documents are received, classified and delivered between state administration bodies, as well as state administration bodies and the General Secretariat of the Government of Montenegro through this system.

186. The eDMS information system provides monitoring in electronic form of documents created in the work of state administration bodies from their preparation, electronic signature, and uploading to another state administration body, as well as receiving, recording, distributing, and other procedures with documents in the state administration body to which they were sent, until archiving (hereinafter: business process).

187. The eDMS information system enables the application of an electronic signature in accordance with current regulations. The eDMS information system is managed, and that system functions in accordance with technical norms and standards for the development and management of information systems.

188. The eDMS information system enables, in accordance with the signature plan, for each document, subject, or procedure to define who is responsible, i.e., who has the right to prepare, change and read documents, as well as to change or delete these rights for a specific document, subject or procedure.

189. Documents, that is, items in the eDMS information system, are classified according to:

(1) the plan of unique classification marks in accordance with the regulations on office business;
(2) the choice of the type of documents or cases, that is, the procedure (administrative, the procedure for the preparation of regulations, etc.);
(3) type of document:
   (a) own—document prepared by the state administration body;
   (b) entry document—a document received by the state administration body;
   (c) output document—a document sent by the state administration body.

190. The Rulebook on Technical Conditions and Security Standards for Access to the Unified System for Electronic Data Exchange ("Official Gazette of Montenegro," No. 108/20 of November 6, 2020) prescribes the technical conditions and security standards that, in order to exchange data through the unified system for electronic data exchange, must be provided, i.e., fulfilled by state bodies, state administration bodies, state agencies, state funds and other holders of public authority and local self-government bodies, local government bodies, special and public services, independent and regulatory bodies and legal and physical persons exercising public authority (hereinafter: other subjects) who keep registers and records within the framework of their jurisdiction in electronic form (hereinafter: electronic registers) and manage their information systems, the appearance and content of the request form for determining the fulfillment of technical conditions and security standards, as well as the appearance and content of the application form for employee access to the unified system for electronic data exchange and the request form for the termination of that access.

191. Legal and natural persons in their capacity as parties submit the electronic document to the competent authorities via e-mail to the unique official address for electronic communication designated by the competent authority for receiving electronic submissions through the electronic registered delivery service to the address for electronic registered delivery designated by the competent authority for receipt. Electronic documents may be utilized or transmitted through electronic methods when permitted by the applicable legal procedure. The competent authority delivers the electronic document to the party at the electronic address, that is, the address for electronic registered delivery, which the party designates for receiving electronic documents or by other electronic means, in accordance with special regulations. Delivery of electronic documents between competent authorities is carried out by e-mail, electronic registered delivery service, or other electronic means in accordance with special regulations.

192. Pursuant to the Law on Electronic Documents ("Official Gazette of Montenegro," No. 132/22 of December 5, 2022), legal and natural persons, i.e., competent authorities, are obliged to store electronic documents in their original form, in an electronic archive, in an information system or on media that enable the durability of the electronic record for the determined storage time, in accordance with the law, i.e., legal work.

193. The electronic archive must ensure that:

(1) electronic documents are stored in the form in which they were created, sent, received, and stored and which does not change the content of the documents;
(2) electronic documents are available in legible form for the entire period of storage to the persons who have the right:
  (a) access to those documents;
  (b) data on electronic signatures, i.e., electronic seals with which electronic documents were signed, are stored, as well as data for checking those electronic signatures, i.e., electronic seals;

(c) electronic documents are stored in the form and by means of technology and procedures which, along with built-in electronic signatures or electronic seals provide a reasonable guarantee for their credibility and integrity for the entire time of storage and that they cannot be changed or deleted without authorization within the time established by law, i.e., by legal act;

(d) for each electronic document, it is possible to reliably determine the origin, creator, time, manner, and form in which it was received into the system for safekeeping;

(e) procedures for maintaining and replacing media for storing electronic documents do not impair the integrity and inviolability of electronic documents.

Chapter 6. Consumer Protection (Online Sales and Online Services)

194. The Directorate for Protection from Computer and Security Incidents on the Internet (Computer Incident Response Team—CIRT) was formed within the MPA.

195. Based on Articles 38 and 41 of the Law on State Administration ("Official Gazette of the Republic of Montenegro," No. 38/03 and Official Gazette of Montenegro Nos. 22/2008, 42/2011, and 54/2016), the Rulebook on the work of this team was adopted on the basis of which the responsibilities of employees are defined, as well as their rights, obligations, and authorizations.

196. The users of the CIRT are as follows: state bodies, state administration bodies, bodies of local self-government units, legal entities with public powers (hereinafter: Authorities), and other legal and physical entities that gain access to or handle data.

197. The CIRT performs the function of protection against computer security incidents on the Internet and other risks related to the information security of its users.

198. CIRT represents the central point of contact (point of contact) at the national and international level for all computer security incidents in which one party to the incident is located in Montenegro (i.e., if it is in the .me domain or in the Montenegrin IP address space).

199. The categorization of the incident is as follows: Offensive content (spam, hate speech, child/sexual violence), malicious code (virus, worm, rootkit, spyware, dialer, rootkit), information gathering (scanning, sniffing, social engineering), intrusion attempts (exploitation known vulnerabilities, login attempts, new attacks) intrusions (privileged account compromise, non-privileged account compromise, application compromise, bot), availability (DoS, DDoS, sabotage, human error), data security (unauthorized data access, unauthorized data modification), fraud (illegal use of resources, copyright, impersonation, phishing), other (all incidents that do not belong to the previous categories).

200. CIRT undertakes measures for:

(1) incident processing, reaction, and coordination in case of incidents;
(2) preparation of security warnings and advice to its users;
(3) raising the level of awareness and educating users.

201. CIRT is not liable for:

(1) operational problem-solving and care for the security of individual systems;
(2) punishing problematic users;

(3) arbitration in disputes (except at the official request of the competent state body);
(4) initiation of criminal charges.

202. CIRT also performs tasks related to:

(1) coordinating the activities of local CIRT teams on the territory of Montenegro;
(2) maintaining contact with other state bodies, legal and natural persons regarding the preservation and improvement of information security;
(3) exchange of information with national teams of other countries through membership in international organizations;
(4) prevention, processing, and elimination of the consequences of computer security incidents on the Internet and other security risks of information systems: in the sense of a proactive way of acting, which includes providing information and assessing the state of information security, checking system vulnerabilities, collecting, recording and processing data about incidents as and testing and application of new software and hardware systems for the protection of IT resources;
(5) data processing and elimination of consequences in terms of determining the occurrence and severity of the incident, determining the cause of the incident, mediation in contacting other parties involved in the incident;
(6) educating users on information security through direct communication and placing publications, manuals, software tools, and other useful information related to safer use of information technologies on the Internet (https://cirt.gov.me);
(7) provision of consulting services to other institutions on information security issues.

203. The Decree on Information Security Measures ("Official Gazette of Montenegro," No. 058/10 of October 8, 2010, 055/15 of September 30, 2015) establishes information security measures that ensure the basic protection of data on physical, technical and organizational level. Pursuant to the Regulation, information security measures of physical protection are determined depending on the type, number, form, and method of storage data, data access authorizations, as well as security assessments of possible risks.

204. Pursuant to the Law on Information Security ("Official Gazette of Montenegro," Nos. 014/10 dated 03/17/2010, 040/16 dated 06/30/2016, 074/20 dated 07/23/2020, 067/21 dated 06/22/2021), information security includes measures for:

(1) physical protection;
(2) data protection;
(3) protection of the information system.

205. In order to improve information security measures, as well as monitor the work and propose activities to the CIRT to establish a system of protection against computer and security incidents on the Internet, the Government of Montenegro is establishing the Council for Information Security.

206. This Council consists of representatives of the state administration body responsible for internal affairs, the state administration body responsible for defense affairs, the state administration body responsible for judicial affairs, the administrative body responsible for the information society, the administrative body responsible for classified information and the National Security Agency (NSA), and representatives of other authorities and institutions, if necessary.

Chapter 7. Liability of Online Service Providers

207. The provider of electronic trust services and the authorities referred to in Article 4 of the LEIES are obliged to apply organizational and technical measures to protect electronic signature certificates, electronic seal certificates and data related to the signatory, as well as the author of the electronic seal, and establish and applies a system of protection of access to records of certificates and revoked and suspended certificates which will allow access only to authorized persons and which provides verification of the accuracy of data transmission and timely insight into possible errors of technical means in accordance with the standards prescribed by the Rulebook on measures and activities for the protection of electronic signature certificates and electronic seal ("Official Gazette of Montenegro," No. 053/18 of July 31, 2018, 020/20 of March 20, 2020).

208. The qualified provider of electronic trust services determines the employees who are responsible for the development and implementation of internal acts and the establishment of a unique system of protection and security of the system of the qualified provider of electronic trust services.

209. A qualified provider of electronic trust services in accordance with Article 34 paragraph 1 point 4 of the LEIES must:

(1) have employed or engaged persons with VI and VII-1 level of education qualification in the field of ICT and work experience of at least three years in the field of maintenance and security of information systems;
(2) have employed or engaged persons with VII-1 level of educational qualifications and five years of work experience in the field of information systems;
(3) have employed or engaged persons with VI and VII-1 level of education qualification in the field of ICT and work experience of at least three years who possess appropriate professional knowledge (completed training, appropriate certificate or work experience);
(4) ensure regular, and at least once a year, attendance at training and seminars in order to update knowledge about current security procedures and new security threats;
(5) ensure that the jobs for which the employee or hired person is in charge are clearly described within the job description established by the act on internal organization and systematization, a special act, or another document and that they are available to employees or hired persons;
(6) ensure that the jobs of employees or persons engaged in the process of providing electronic trust services are clearly delineated in accordance with job descriptions determined by the act on internal organization and systematization, a special act, or another document.

210. A qualified provider of electronic trust services ensures that it has employees with specialist knowledge, experience, and professional qualifications required to provide electronic trust services in accordance with the standards: ETSI EN 319 401, ETSI EN 319 411-1, ETSI EN 319 411-2 and ETSI EN 319 421.

211. Pursuant to Article 3 of the Rulebook on minimum technical standards and accompanying procedures in relation to which the degree of security of the electronic identification system is determined ("Official Gazette of Montenegro," No. 053/18, dated July 31, 2018, 020/20 of March 20, 2018), the degree of security of the means of electronic identification is determined, based on the verification of essential elements in the electronic identification system.

212. The check includes procedures and activities during which:

(1) enrollment checks:
  - completeness and accuracy of the data in the user's request for the issuance of electronic identification means;
  - user registration when issuing means of electronic identification;
  - the reliability and quality of proving and verifying the identity of a natural person as a user;
  - the reliability and quality of proving and verifying the identity of a legal entity as a user;
  - reliability and quality of connection by means of electronic identification of legal entities and natural persons authorized to represent a legal entity.

(2) management of electronic identification means checking reliability and quality:
  - characteristics and design of means of electronic identification;
  - issuance, delivery, and activation of means of electronic identification;
  - suspension, revocation, and reactivation of means of electronic identification;
  - renewal and replacement of means of electronic identification.

(3) authentication is checked by the reliability and quality of the authentication mechanism;

(4) management and organization checks reliability and quality:
  - internal acts on the manner and procedures of issuing means of electronic identification;
  - public notification and user information;
  - information security management;
  - keeping records of issued means of electronic identification;
  - premises and employees who are related to the electronic identification system;
  - technical controls carried out by a natural person, a legal entity, or the authority that issues the funds;
  - electronic identification;
  - compliance and audits of the electronic identification system.

213. In addition to the above, according to the LEIES (Article 34), a qualified electronic trust service provider must meet the following conditions:

(1) has an updated plan for terminating the provision of the electronic trust service in order to ensure its continuity, which it adopts in accordance with the internal acts from Article 37, paragraph 4 of this law;
(2) ensure the processing of personal data in accordance with regulations on the protection of personal data;
(3) provide, in an appropriate manner and in accordance with this law and the internal acts from Article 37 paragraph 4 of this law, the verification of the identity of the signatory and, if necessary, other characteristics of the natural and legal person, who are issued a qualified certificate for electronic signature, i.e., a qualified certificate for electronic seal;
(4) has employed persons with specialist knowledge, experience, and professional qualifications required for the provision of electronic trust services, especially in relation to abilities at the management level, expertise in the application of administrative procedures;
(5) uses reliable systems and products that are protected against unauthorized changes and that provide technical and cryptographic process security;
(6) undertakes measures to prevent forgery of certificates, and in cases where it creates data for the creation of an electronic signature, guarantees the confidentiality of the process of creating such data and delivers certificates to signatories in a secure manner;
(7) has financial resources for risk and liability insurance for possible damage caused by the issuance of qualified certificates, in an amount that can cover the risk of damage and liability caused by the use of qualified certificates issued by him, if the signatory is not responsible for the damage or has concluded an insurance contract from risks and responsibilities for that type of damage;
(8) has a system for storing all relevant data related to qualified certificates in a certain period of time, especially for the purpose of providing such data from the records of qualified certificates for the needs of the court and other legal proceedings, whereby such data can also be stored in electronic form, in the manner which enables verification of electronic signatures;
(9) uses a reliable system for storing qualified certificates in a form that enables verification in order to:
    (a) data entry and changes during the provision of electronic trust services are performed only by authorized persons;
    (b) the authenticity of the data from the qualified certificate could be checked;
    (c) the data was publicly available for searching in a fast and safe way only in those cases for which it is approved by the registered signatory;
    (d) any technical change, which could violate safety requirements, was visible to a qualified person electronic trust service provider.

Part IV. Intellectual Rights ("Digital Rights")

214. Montenegro is a signatory to important international treaties in the area of intellectual property, including which consists of:

- Convention on the Establishment of the World Intellectual Property Organization—Regulation on ratification of the Convention on the Establishment of the World Intellectual Property Organization ("Official Gazette of the SFRY—International Treaties and Other Agreements," No. 31/72 and "Official Gazette of the SFRY—International Treaties," No. 4/86).
- Paris Convention for the Protection of Industrial Property—Regulation on ratification of the Paris Convention for the Protection of Industrial Property ("Official Gazette of the SFRY—International Treaties and Other Agreements," No. 5/74 and "Official Gazette of the SFRY—International Treaties," No. 7/86).
- Berne Convention for the Protection of Literary and Artistic Works—Law on Ratification of the Berne Convention for the Protection of Literary and Artistic Works ("Official Journal of the SFRY—International Treaties," No. 14/75).
- Madrid Agreement on the Suppression of False and Fraudulent Indications of Origin on Products—Law on Ratification of the Madrid Agreement on the Elimination of False and Fraudulent Indications of Origin on Products ("Official Gazette of the FRY—International Treaties," No. 1/99).
- Madrid Agreement on the International Registration of Trademarks—Regulation on Ratification of the Madrid Agreement on the International Registration of Trademarks ("Official Gazette of the SFRY—International Treaties and Other Agreements," No. 2/74).
- Protocol Relating to the Madrid Arrangement Concerning the International Registration of Trademarks—Law on the Confirmation of the Protocol relating to the Madrid Arrangement Concerning the International Registration of Marks ("Official Gazette of the FRY—International Treaties," No. 2/97).
- The Hague Agreement Concerning the International Reporting of Industrial Samples and Models (Hague Document) and the Stockholm Supplementary Act—Law on the Ratification of the Hague Agreement Concerning the International Reporting of Industrial Samples and Models (The Hague Document) and the Stockholm Supplementary Act ("Official Gazette of the FRY—International Treaties," No. 3/93).

- Locarno Agreement Establishing an International Classification for Industrial Samples and Models—Law on Ratification of the Locarno Arrangement Establishing an International Classification for Industrial Samples and Models ("Official Gazette of the SFRY—International Treaties and Other Agreements," No. 51/74).
- Lisbon Agreement on the Protection of Designations of Origin and their International Registration—Law on the Confirmation of the Lisbon Agreement on the Protection of Designations of Origin and their International Registration ("Official Gazette of the FRY—International Treaties," No. 6/98).
- Nairobi Agreement on the Protection of the Olympic Symbol, with annex—Law on the Confirmation of the Nairobi Treaty on the Protection of the Olympic Symbol, with an annex ("Official Gazette of the FRY—International Treaties," No. 1/99).
- Trademark Law Treaty—Law on the Ratification of the Trademark Law Treaty ("Official Gazette of the FRY—International Treaties," No. 4/98).
- WIPO Copyright Treaty—Law on Ratification of WIPO Copyright Treaties ("Official Gazette of fry—International Treaties," No. 13/02).
- WIPO Treaty on Interpretations and Phonograms—Law on Ratification of the WIPO Treaty on Interpretations and Phonograms ("Official Gazette of the FRY—International Treaties," No. 13/02).
- Budapest Agreement Concerning the International Recognition of the Deposit of Microorganisms for the Purposes of Patenting Procedure—Act on the Ratification of the Budapest Agreement Concerning the International Recognition of the Deposit of Microorganisms for The Purpose of Patenting Procedure ("Official Gazette of the FRY—International Treaties," No. 3/93).
- Agreement on Cooperation in the Field of Patents, with the Rulebook for the Implementation of the Patent Cooperation Agreement—Law on Confirmation of the Patent Cooperation Agreement, with the Rulebook for the Implementation of the Patent Cooperation Agreement ("Official Gazette of the FRY—International Treaties," No. 3/96 and "Official Gazette of Serbia," No. 32/04).
- Convention on the Distribution of Programme Signals transmitted by Satellite—Regulation on ratification of the Convention on the Distribution of Programme Signals transmitted by Satellite ("Official Gazette of the SFRY—International Treaties," No. 13/77).
- International Convention for the Protection of Contractors, Producers of Phonograms and Broadcasting Institutions—Law on Ratification of the International Convention for the Protection of Contractors, Producers of Phonograms and Broadcasting Institutions ("Official Gazette of the FRY—International Treaties," No. 13/02).
- Convention on the Protection of Producers of Phonograms against Unauthorized Duplication of Their Phonograms—Law on the Protection of Producers of Phonograms against Unauthorized Duplication of Their Phonograms ("Official Gazette of the FRY—International Treaties," No. 13/02).[137]

137. Intellectual Property Strategy of Montenegro for the Period 2022–2025.

215. In addition to the above international treaties, in Montenegro are also in force:

- Patent Law Treaty—Law on the Ratification of the Treaty on Patent Law ("Official Gazette of Montenegro—International Treaties," No. 14/11).
- Nice Agreement Concerning the International Classification of Goods and Services for the Registration of Trademarks—Law on the Confirmation of the Nice Agreement Concerning the International Classification of Goods and Services for the Registration of Marks of June 15, 1957, revised at Stockholm on July 14, 1967, and Geneva on May 13, 1977, with amendment of September 28, 1979 ("Official Gazette of Montenegro—International Treaties," No. 9/12).
- Strasbourg Agreement on the International Patent Classification—Law on the Ratification of the Strasbourg Agreement Concerning the International Classification of Patents ("Official Gazette of Montenegro—International Treaties" No. 14/11).
- Vienna Agreement Establishing the International Classification of Figurative Elements of Trademarks, adopted in Vienna on 12 June and amended on October 1, 1985—Vienna Agreement on the Establishment of the International Classification of Figurative Elements of Trademarks ("Official Gazette of Montenegro —International Treaties" No. 08/11).
- International Convention for the Protection of New Varieties of Plants—Law on Ratification of the International Convention for the Protection of New Varieties of Plants ("Official Gazette of Montenegro—International Treaties," No. 4/13).
- Geneva Act of the Hague Agreement on the International Registration of Industrial Designs—Law on Ratification of the Geneva Act of the Hague Agreement on the International Registration of Industrial Designs ("Official Gazette of Montenegro—International Treaties," No. 8/11).
- Agreement on Trade-Related Aspects of Intellectual Property Rights—Law on Ratification of the Protocol on the Accession of Montenegro to the Marrakesh Agreement on the Establishment of the World Trade Organization ("Official Gazette of Montenegro—International Treaties," No. 3/12).
- Agreement between the Government of Montenegro and the European Patent Organization on the Extension of European Patents (Enlargement Agreement)—Law on Confirmation of the Agreement between the Government of Montenegro and the European Patent Organization on the Extension of European Patents (Enlargement Agreement), (Official Gazette of Montenegro —International Treaties" No. 5/09).[138]

216. At the national level, the legal framework regarding intellectual property includes:

- Law on Copyright and Related Rights ("Official Gazette of Montenegro," Nos. 37/11 53/160, 145/21).
- Law on Optical Discs ("Official Gazette of Montenegro" No. 02/07 and "Official Gazette of Montenegro," Nos. 73/10 and 53/11).

138. *Ibid.*

- Patent Law ("Official Gazette of Montenegro," Nos. 42/15, 2/17, 146/21).
- Trademark Law ("Official Gazette of Montenegro," Nos. 72/10, 44/12, 18/14, 40/16, and 2/17).
- Law on Geographical Indications ("Official Gazette of Montenegro," Nos. 48/08 and 40/11).
- Law on the Legal Protection of Industrial Designs ("Official Gazette of Montenegro," Nos. 80/10, 27/13. 42/16 and 2/17).
- Law on the Protection of Semiconductor Topography ("Official Gazette of Montenegro," Nos. 75/10 and 40/16).
- Law on the Protection of Plant Varieties ("Official Gazette of Montenegro," Nos. 48/07, 48/08 and 40/11).
- Law on the Protection of Unpublished Data ("Official Gazette of Montenegro," no. 16/07 and 73/08).
- Law on the Application of Regulations Governing the Protection of Intellectual Property Rights ("Official Gazette of the RCG," No. 45/05 and "Official Gazette of Montenegro," Nos. 73/10, 37/11, 40/11, 18/14, 42/15 and 42/16).
- Criminal Code ("Official Gazette of Montenegro," Nos. 70/03, 13/04, 47/06 40/08, 25/10, 73/10, 32/11, 64/11, 40/13, 56/13, 14/15, 42/15, 58/15, 44/17, 49/18 and 3/20)—Chapter twenty-first—Crimes against intellectual property.[139]

217. For the purposes of this entry, it is important to note that not all these legal sources contain specific norms for ICT products. Depending on a product, in some cases, their general provisions do not apply either. The chapters below will focus on those regulatory frameworks that are applicable in ICT, either through their general or specific provisions. For the others, we advise consulting specific encyclopedic entries for that specific field of law.

139. *Ibid.*

Chapter 1. Patent Law

218. One of the IP rights that is usually discussed in relation to the protection of products in the ICT sector is patents. According to the Montenegrin Law on Patents,[140] a patent provides legal protection to an invention in any field of technology, subject to the invention being novel, innovative, and industrially applicable.[141] The usual object of a patent is a product, such as a device or a process.[142] However, computer programs are explicitly excluded from the patenting process. Article 5(5) of the Law on Patents lists certain devices and processes that are not to be considered innovations, and these are:

(1) discoveries, scientific theories, and mathematical methods;
(2) aesthetic creations;
(3) plans, rules, and procedures for the performance of intellectual activities, for playing games or for performing tasks;
(4) computer programs;
(5) displaying information.

140. "Službeni list Crne Gore," br. 042/15 od 29.07.2015, 002/17 od 10.01.2017, 146/21 od 31.12.2021.
141. Article 5(1) of the Law on Patents.
142. Article 5(2) of the Law on Patents.

Chapter 2. Copyright Protection in the Digital Context

219. Copyright and related rights are governed by the Law on Copyright and Related Rights[143] (hereinafter: "Copyright Law") adopted on July 27, 2011. The Copyright Law was amended several times after it entered into force, and it governs several aspects of the works in the area of ICT. Software, or computer programs, are regarded as works of authorship under the Copyright Law (Article 3 of the Copyright Law). This section will discuss several general provisions in the Law that explicitly deal with software (either by making a specific comment about the software or excluding it from its applicability) as well as the Law's special section on computer programs.

220. The protection of copyright is governed by Article 4 of the Copyright Law. It defines any individual intellectual creation in the domains of literature, science, and art as a copyrighted work, regardless of its kind, mode, or form of expression, unless otherwise stated in the Law. The article also specifies that copyrighted works include literary texts, studies, manuals, articles, and other forms of writing, as well as computer programs. This means that individuals who develop computer programs through coding are generally protected as copyright holders.

221. Other types of ICT works are discussed in the Copyright Law as well. Article 7(1) of the Copyright Law governs the protection of "a collection of copyrighted works or other materials (encyclopedias, anthologies, databases, collections of documents, etc.), which, considering the selection or harmonization or arrangement of contents," may be considered a spiritual creation in the field of literature, science, and art, which is expressed in a certain way. In particular, the databases referred to in this paragraph of Article 7 are considered the collections of independent works, data, or other material in any form, arranged according to the system or method and individually accessible by electronic or other means. This would include the protection of electronic databases as a separate protection of ICT works from copyright, as will be discussed below. However, according to Article 7(4), "the protection of a collection under this Law does not include computer programs used for the creation or operation of electronic databases."

§1. General Provisions in the Copyright Law that Deal Specifically with the Software

I. Moral Rights of the Author

222. Article 14(1) of the Copyright Law defines moral rights as those that protect the author's spiritual and personal connections with the work. The author, for example, has the exclusive right to determine whether, when, where, and how his

143. "Službeni list Crne Gore," br. 037/11 od 29.07.2011, 053/16 od 11.08.2016, 145/21 od 31.12.2021.

work will be published for the first time.[144] Authors have the exclusive right to be recognized as author of their work in such a way that their names is indicated in the work and in connection with their work, and they may determine that their right of authorship is indicated in another way.[145] The author shall have the exclusive right to oppose any modification or use of the work if such modification or use would be harmful to her or his honor or reputation.[146]

223. Furthermore, Article 18 of the Copyright Law allows the author to revoke in writing the assigned economic right in the work from the holder of such rights if there are serious moral reasons for doing so and provided that the author compensates the right older for the actual damage caused.

II. Economic and Other Rights of the Author

224. Article 19(1) and (2) of the Copyright Law provides that the economic rights of the author give the author exclusive power to prohibit or authorize the exploitation of the work and copies thereof. The exploitation of a copyrighted work is permitted only when the author grants the corresponding economic rights in the work unless otherwise provided by the Copyright Law or contract.[147] For each use of the copyrighted work by another person, the author shall be entitled to a fee—honorarium, i.e., fair compensation, unless otherwise stipulated by this Law or contract.[148]

225. In terms of the substance of economic rights, Article 20 of the Copyright Law provides that these contain in particular:

(1) the right of reproduction;
(2) the right of distribution;
(3) the right to lease;
(4) the right to give service;
(5) the right of public performance;
(6) the right to communicate publicly from phonograms or videograms;
(7) the right of public display;
(8) the right to broadcast;
(9) the right of retransmission;
(10) the right of cable retransmission;
(11) the right to publicly communicate the work to be broadcast;
(12) the right to another public communication;
(13) the right to make the work available to the public;
(14) the right to work;

144. Article 15(1) of the Copyright Law.
145. Article 16(1) and (2) of the Copyright Law.
146. Article 17(1) of the Copyright Law.
147. Article 19(3) of the Copyright Law.
148. Article 19(4) of the Copyright Law.

(15) the right of audiovisual adaptation.

226. Other rights of the author under the Copyright Law are the right of access to work,[149] the right to remuneration for resale of their artwork,[150] and the right to remuneration of sound or visual recording or photocopying of his work.[151]

III. Substantive Limitations to Copyright

227. There are several types of copyright infringement that can appear in the case of computer program. These infringements are known as piracy, and they include a spectrum of conduct, such as:

- multiple installations;
- end-user piracy;
- client/server piracy;
- online piracy.[152]

228. However, in some cases provided by law, the copyright can be circumvented.

229. For example, Article 45(1) of the Copyright Law states that substantive limitations to copyright shall be possible only in such cases as are stipulated in the Law, if they are not contrary to the normal exploitation of the work and if this does not cause unreasonable harm to the legitimate interests of the author. These limitations are not waivable, and the user is obliged to indicate the source and author of the work when they are applicable.[153]

230. The limitations governed by the Copyright Law are:

- statutory license; and
- free use.

231. The latter contains specific provisions regarding ICT-related copyright.

232. When it comes to **statutory license**, the Copyright Law prescribes two situations in which one might use a copyrighted work without acquiring copyright but by paying adequate compensation. The first type of situation, as governed under Article 46 of the Copyright Law, includes:

149. Article 33 of the Copyright Law.
150. Articles 34 and 35 of the Copyright Law.
151. Articles 36–38 of the Copyright Law.
152. Ian J. Lloyd, *Information Technology Law* (9th edn, Oxford University Press 2017) 337.
153. Article 45(2)–(4) of the Copyright Law.

(1) using parts of the published copyright work only for illustrations for the purpose of teaching according to a public education program or scientific research, in reading books and textbooks, which unite the works of several authors;
(2) using individually published works in the field of photography, fine art, architecture, applied arts, industrial design, and cartography only for illustration for the purpose of teaching according to a public education program or scientific research, in reading books and textbooks, which combine the works of several authors;
(3) copying in print media or in the form of a press review (clipping) of published articles, broadcast works, and works of a similar character on current economic, political, or religious issues, if those rights are not expressly reserved.

233. The second type of situation includes copying and broadcasting copyrighted work within public institutions, such as student dormitories, hospitals, or prisons, if it is carried out without direct or indirect material gain and the due compensation is paid.[154]

234. When it comes to **free use**, there are several limitations of copyright based on such use provided in the Copyright Law:

(1) Under conditions prescribed in Article 48 of the Copyright Law (the need to adapt the work to the required form and using it for no profit), it is allowed to use the copyrighted work for the needs of persons with disabilities without acquiring the appropriate copyright and without paying compensation.
(2) Under conditions prescribed in Article 49 of the Copyright Law, it is permissible, without acquiring copyright and without paying compensation, to temporarily copy the copyrighted work.
(3) Under Article 50 of the Copyright Law, it is permissible, without acquiring copyright and without paying compensation, to share copyrighted work to the extent justified by the purpose of informing (e.g., when notifying daily events, preparing and copying summaries of published newspaper or similar articles in the form of a press review, using political speeches, as well as excerpts from public lectures and similar acts).
(4) Under conditions prescribed in Article 51 of the Copyright Law, it is allowed, without acquiring copyright and without paying compensation, for the purpose of education and upbringing (preschool and school classes, research, exams), and without achieving a direct or indirect material gain.
(5) Under conditions prescribed in Article 52 of the Copyright Law, it is permitted, without copyright and without paying compensation, to copy the published work:

154. Article 47 of the Copyright Law.

- A physical person may copy the work on paper or other similar means using an appropriate photographic technique or other procedure with similar effects or on another means if the copying is carried out for private use, if the copies are not available to the public and if the copying is not carried out for direct or indirect material gain.
- Public archives, libraries, museums, and educational or research institutions may copy the work onto any means, if the impotence is carried out from a copy owned by that legal entity for internal use and provided that it is not carried out for direct or indirect material gain.

(6) Under conditions prescribed in Article 53 of the Copyright Law, it is permissible, without acquiring copyright and without paying compensation, to use a quotation from the published work in another work, if the quotation is used for criticism, confirmation, or reference if it is done in accordance with fair practice and is carried out to the extent necessary for that purpose.

(7) Under conditions prescribed in Article 53a of the Copyright Law, it is allowed to use copyrighted works during celebrations organized by a state authority or competent authority of a city, capital, or local self-government unit, i.e., local government body, on the occasion of holidays established by the law regulating state and other holidays, without acquiring copyright and without paying compensation, if the use of these acts does not result in direct or indirect material gain.

(8) Under conditions prescribed in Article 54 of the Copyright Law, it is allowed, without acquiring copyright and without paying compensation, to use a published copyrighted work for the purpose of public safety, as well as to conduct proceedings before judicial or other state bodies and in arbitration.

(9) Under conditions prescribed in Article 55 of the Copyright Law, it is permissible, without acquiring copyright and without paying compensation, to use works that are permanently exhibited in parks, on streets, squares, and other public spaces.

(10) Under conditions prescribed in Article 56 of the Copyright Law, a published work which is accidentally included in another work or which is of secondary importance in relation to another work may, when using that work, it can be used without acquiring copyright and without paying compensation.

(11) Under conditions prescribed in Article 57 of the Copyright Law, the organizer of a public exhibition or public sale of works of art may, without acquiring copyright and without paying compensation, use those works for the purpose and to the extent necessary for the advertising and promotion of such events, without direct or indirect material gain.

(12) Under conditions prescribed in Article 58 of the Copyright Law, it is permissible, without acquiring copyright and without paying compensation, to imitate the published work (e.g., the work has been imitated for the purposes of creating a parody, caricature or pastiche, if this does not cause confusion as to the source of the work).

(13) Article 59 of the Copyright Law provides that in the facilities where phonograms are repaired or sold, videograms and devices for their use or receipt, one may copy or show to the public copyrighted work, without acquiring

copyright and without paying compensation, to the extent necessary for the demonstration and repair of phonograms, videograms, and other specified devices.

(14) Article 60 of the Copyright Law provides that natural persons may, for the purpose of research or personal learning, use copyrighted works through certain terminals in the premises of archives and libraries, museums, and educational or scientific institutions from their collections without acquiring copyright and without paying compensation, if the use of these works is not conditional on purchase or licensing.

(15) Under conditions prescribed in Article 61 of the Copyright Law, a lawful user of a published database or a copy thereof may, without acquiring copyright and without paying compensation, use that database if necessary for access and customary use of its contents.

235. One of the examples of regulation of free use refers to computer programs explicitly. As mentioned above, under conditions prescribed in Article 52 of the Copyright Law, it is permitted, without copyright and without paying compensation, to copy the copyrighted published work. Still, in certain cases, free use is forbidden despite the condition described above being met. Such reproduction shall not be permitted if the reproduction is done in the volume of an entire book, musical sheet music, electronic databases, or computer programs, as well as the construction of architectural objects according to the design and on the basis of copies that have been unlawfully copied or made available to the public.[155]

IV. Work Created During Employment

236. Article 100 of the Copyright Law governs the copyright in works created under employment contracts: If an author created a copyrighted work in the course of employment and the performance of their work obligations or following the instructions of the employer, it is considered that all economic and other rights of the author in that work are without any limitations and exclusively transferred to the employer for a period of five years from the creation of the work unless otherwise specified in the contract. Paragraph 2 of Article 100 prescribes that after the expiration of the deadline of five years, the economic and other rights in this work shall be acquired by the author. Still, the author will be under obligation to, at the request of the employer, hand over the economic and other rights in that work for appropriate remuneration.[156]

237. There are certain exceptions reserved for the authors of collected works and databases. Article 101(1) of the Copyright Law states that the author reserves the right to use the work created during the employment when publishing his or her collected works. Also, the same article provides that the economic rights of the author

155. Article 52(2) of the Copyright Law.
156. Article 100(3) of the Copyright Law.

and other rights of the author in a database and in a collective work shall be deemed to have been exclusively and unlimitedly transferred to the employer unless otherwise provided by the contract.[157]

238. These rules have a few exceptions governed by law. One is in relation to computer programs. Article 115 of the Copyright Law prescribes that if the computer program is made in the course of employment or on the basis of a service contract, all property and other rights of the author in that program are unlimitedly and exclusively transferred to the employer or a person who ordered the program unless otherwise specified in the contract. Similarly, if the database is created during employment or on the basis of a service contract, all economic rights on that database shall be deemed to be exclusively and indefinitely transferred to the employer or contracting authority, unless otherwise stipulated in the contract.[158]

§2. Special Provisions Regarding Copyright on Computer Programs

239. The Copyright Law contains special provisions regarding copyright on computer programs in Articles 110–115. These provisions, however, do not affect the rights acquired and exercised on the basis of regulations on patents, trademarks, unfair competition, trade secrets, protection of semiconductor topography, and contract law on computer programs.[159] For the purposes of the Copyright Law, a computer program, i.e., software, is a written author's work expressed in all forms, including design material for its creation.[160] The software still needs to meet the criteria of being an "individual intellectual creation in the domains of literature, science, and art," as per Article 4 of the Copyright Law. There are elements of the development process of a computer program that are excluded from this copyright, and these are the ideas, principles, procedures, and methods that are the basis for the creation of a computer program, as well as for its interface.[161]

240. In terms of limitations on copyright, the Copyright Law prescribes a limitation specific to computer programs. It states that a person who has the right to use a computer program may, without the permission of the author:

(1) make one backup copy of the program, if necessary, for its use;
(2) monitor, investigate, and test the functioning of the program in order to inspect the ideas and principles that underlie the elements of the functioning, operation, transmission, and recording of the program for which it is authorized.[162]

157. Article 101(2) of the Copyright Law.
158. Article 141(2) of the Copyright Law.
159. Article 110 of the Copyright Law.
160. Article 111(1) of the Copyright Law.
161. Article 111(2) of the Copyright Law.
162. Article 113(2) of the Copyright Law.

241. These limitations cannot be contractually waived, as such a provision would be found null and void.[163]

242. Furthermore, the duplication of the code of a computer program and the translation of its form may be carried out without acquiring copyright and without payment of compensation, if the reproduction or translation is carried out for the purpose of obtaining the necessary data to achieve interoperability of independently created programs with other programs or computer equipment.[164] In order to do this legally, a certain set of conditions need to be met:

(1) reproduction or translation is carried out by a person who, in accordance with the law, has the right to use a computer program;
(2) the data for achieving interoperability has not been previously and easily accessible to the person referred to in point 1 of this paragraph;
(3) those actions are limited only to the parts of the program which are necessary to achieve interoperability.[165]

243. The information and data obtained by performing these actions referred shall not be:

(1) used for purposes other than to achieve interoperability of an independently created computer program;
(2) communicated to other persons, unless this is necessary for the interoperability of an independently created computer program;
(3) used for the development, production, or placement of another computer program that is substantially similar to the computer program referred to in paragraph 1 of this Article or for another action that may infringe copyright.[166]

244. Contractual stipulations waiving these restrictions are to be found null and void.[167]

163. Article 113(4) of the Copyright Law.
164. Article 114(1) of the Copyright Law.
165. *Ibid.*
166. Article 114(2) of the Copyright Law.
167. Article 114(4) of the Copyright Law.

Chapter 3. Protection of Databases (Incl. "Data Ownership")

245. The Copyright Law governs other ICT works besides computer programs. One of them is databases. Article 139 of the Copyright Law states that a database manufacturer who demonstrates that they made a substantial qualitative and/or quantitative investment in the acquisition, verification, or presentation of the contents of the database shall have the right to prohibit the extraction and/or re-use of the contents of the database as a whole or of its qualitatively and/or quantitatively substantial part. There are two exceptions to this prohibition. First, public service will not be considered an action to extract or reuse the contents of a database; second, such prohibition of extraction and/or reuse of the contents does not apply to computer programs used for the creation or operation of electronic databases.[168]

246. The rights defined above shall apply to databases whose providers or copyright holders are citizens of Montenegro or have their place of residence on the territory of Montenegro, or they are companies established in accordance with the laws and regulations of Montenegro and which have a registered seat or principal place of business in Montenegro.[169]

247. They will also apply to databases whose providers or copyright holders are nationals of a Member State of the EU, have their place of residence on the territory of the EU, or are companies established in accordance with the law regulations of a Member State of the EU and which have a registered headquarters, headquarters, or principal place of business in the EU.

248. In any case, if a company is a database provider in either of these cases, it should have its registered office in the territory of Montenegro or the EU, and its activity must be actually and permanently connected with the economy of Montenegro or a Member State of the EU.[170]

249. According to Article 142 of the Copyright Law, after the first sale of a copy of a database by a copyright holder or with her or his consent in the territory of Montenegro, or in the Territory of the EU or the Member States of the European Economic Area, the copyright holder's right to control the resale of that copy in those territories is considered exhausted.[171]

250. Furthermore, the provider of a database that was made available to the public is not allowed to prevent a lawful user of that database or part of the contents of the database from extracting and/or reusing qualitatively or quantitatively irrelevant parts of the database.[172] At the same time, such a lawful user of a database made

168. Article 139(5) and (6) of the Copyright Law.
169. Article 145a(1) and (2) of the Copyright Law.
170. Article 145a(3) and (6) of the Copyright Law.
171. Article 145a(4) and (5) of the Copyright Law.
172. Article 143(1) of the Copyright Law.

available to the public or copies thereof is prohibited from performing actions contrary to the usual exploitation of the database, which causes unreasonable harm to the legitimate interests of the provider.[173] The lawful user of such a database is also not allowed to infringe the copyright or related rights in a work or subject of protection that is part of that database.[174] All these forbearances cannot be waived by a contract; such contractual stipulations will be considered null and void.[175]

251. Article 144 of the Copyright Law goes even further by clarifying that a lawful user of a database made available to the public may, without the database provider's permission, extract or reuse an essential part of the contents of that database in the event of extraction:

(1) the contents of a non-electronic database for private purposes;
(2) intended to be shown in teaching or scientific research, indicating the source and to the extent justified by a non-commercial purpose;
(3) and/or re-use for the purposes of public security or administrative or judicial proceedings.

252. These protections of the right of the database provider last from the date of creation of the database until January 1 of the year following the expiration of fifteen years from that date.[176] If the database is made available to the public within that period, then the protection of the rights of the database provider shall last until January 1 of the year following the expiry of fifteen years from the date on which the database was first published.[177] It is important to note that any substantial qualitative or quantitative change in the content of the database shall be subject to a new protection period of fifteen years.[178]

173. Article 143(2) of the Copyright Law.
174. Article 143(3) of the Copyright Law.
175. Article 143(4) of the Copyright Law.
176. Article 145(1) of the Copyright Law.
177. Article 145(2) of the Copyright Law.
178. Article 145(3) of the Copyright Law.

Chapter 4. Chips Protection

253. The Law on the Protection of Topographies of Integrated Circuits of Montenegro (hereinafter: "Law on Topographies of Integrated Circuits") was adopted in 2010 and amended in 2016.[179] The law regulates the conditions for the protection of semiconductor topography and the rights of creators and holders of protected topography.[180]

254. The right to protect the topography of semiconductors (hereinafter: "topography") belongs to its creator.

255. Article 3(1) of the Law on Topographies of Integrated Circuits defines a semiconductor as "a finished product or semi-finished product intended to perform an electronic function, which in a piece of material includes one or more connected layers consisting of integrated elements, of which at least one element is active." The same Article in paragraph 2 defines topography as "a unique set of three-dimensionally related images for each layer recorded or encoded in any way from which a semiconductor is assembled."

256. Article 2(1) of the Law on Topographies of Integrated Circuits states that the right to protection of topography belongs to all creators. If the topography was created during the employment relationship of the creator or on the basis of an order, the right to protection is vested in the employer of the creator or the person who ordered the creation of the topography unless otherwise specified in the contract.[181]

257. The right to protection is obtained through the registration process, and it lasts for ten years as of the submission of the application.[182] The registration process is governed by the Law on Topographies of Integrated Circuits and, in more detail, by the Rulebook on the Content of the Application for the Entry of Topography in the Register of Topography and the Content of the Topography Register.[183]

179. "Službeni list Crne Gore," br. 075/10 od 21.12.2010, 040/16 od 30.06.2016.
180. Article 1 of the Law on Topographies of Integrated Circuits.
181. Article 2(2) of the Law on Topographies of Integrated Circuits.
182. Articles 10(1) and 2(2) of the Law on Topographies of Integrated Circuits.
183. "Službeni list Crne Gore," br. 014/16 od 26.02.2016.

Chapter 5. Protection of Internet Domain Names

258. The registration of internet domain names in Montenegro is governed by the Rulebook on the Procedure of Registration and Using Domains under the National Internet Domain of Montenegro ".me"[184] (hereinafter: "Rulebook on Domains"), and the Decision on the Use of the National Internet Domain of Montenegro ".me" (hereinafter: "Decision on Domain").[185] The Rulebook on Domains prescribes the procedure of registration and use of domains under the national Internet domain of Montenegro ".me."[186] Article 4(3) and (4) of the Rulebook states that the domain is activated after the conclusion of the contract in accordance with the conditions set by the registration agent in accordance with the recommendations of ICANN/IANA.[187] Data on the registered domain and domain user are entered into the registry.[188]

259. The Decision on Domain defines the national Internet domain ".me" to be the basis of Montenegro's recognition on the Internet and an inseparable part of the global Internet community, and as such, is to be used in accordance with the Decision.[189] The domain under the national internet domain ".me" can be used by legal entities and natural persons under equal conditions while respecting the rights and interests of all users in the global Internet community in accordance with international standards.[190]

184. "Službeni list Crne Gore," br. 043/14 od 15.10.2014, 067/18 od 17.10.2018.
185. "Službeni list Crne Gore," br. 050/14 od 28.11.2014.
186. Article 1 of the Rulebook on Domains.
187. Internet Corporation for Assigned Names and Numbers/ Internet Assigned Numbers Authority.
188. Article 4(5) of the Rulebook on Domains.
189. Article 1 of the Decision on Domain.
190. Article 2 of the Decision on Domain.

Part V. Cybersecurity Law

Chapter 1. Institutional Framework (Cybersecurity Agency, National CIRT, Etc.)

260. Over the past decades, Montenegro has established an organizational structure in the field of cybersecurity and identified the state administration bodies responsible for this area, strategic planning, and the implementation of policies defined by previous cybersecurity strategies.

261. CIRT[191] is the CIRT in the cyberspace of Montenegro. The Government of Montenegro and the ITU established it in 2012 as part of their joint project. In accordance with the Law on Classified Information (LCI)[192] and the LIS,[193] it performs the function of protecting against computer security incidents on the Internet and other risks related to information security. Article 11 of the LIS defines the jurisdiction of CIRT as follows:

262. Establishing a system for protecting against computer security incidents on the Internet and other security risks of information systems of organizations and other legal and natural persons.

263. Prevention of computer security incidents. Mitigation of consequences in the case of security incidents on the Internet that extend beyond the scope of information systems of organizations and other legal and natural persons.

264. The National CIRT represents the central contact point at the national and international levels for all computer security incidents in which one of the parties involved is in Montenegro (or if it occurs within Montenegrin IP address space). The authorities and other legal entities to which the LIS applies are obliged to designate individuals responsible for establishing systems for protecting against computer and security incidents on the Internet and other security risks of those systems.

191. CIRT in cyberspace of Montenegro—CIRT.ME.
192. Law on Classified Information of Montenegro ("Official Gazette of Montenegro," Nos. 014/08 from 29.02.2008, 076/09 from 18.11.2009, 041/10 from 23.07.2010, 040/11 from 08.08.2011, 038/12 from 19.07.2012, 044/12 from 09.08.2012, 014/13 from 15.03.2013, 018/14 from 11.04.2014, 048/15 from 21.08.2015, 074/20 from 23.07.2020).
193. Law on Information Security of Montenegro ("Official Gazette of Montenegro," Nos. 14/2010 and 40/2016).

These designated individuals will collaborate directly with CIRT to ensure the harmonization of actions by those authorities and legal entities in implementing information security measures. As part of its daily activities, CIRT performs coordination and response tasks for incident situations in the Montenegrin cyberspace. Incidents are reported online through the website portal www.cirt.me, through the portal www.euprava.me, and via email at kontakt@cirt.me.

265. Since its establishment, there has been a constant increase in the number of incidents reported to CIRT, which highlights the need for further strengthening of the capacity of this body to respond to emerging circumstances. Throughout 2022, the National CIRT implemented proactive and reactive measures aimed at reducing the risk of incidents. The National CIRT continued to develop cooperation with institutions outside of Montenegro, such as other CERT teams, EU and NATO institutions, as well as other institutions within the country, all with the goal of advancing common interests in the field of cybersecurity. Based on the analysis of the current situation, it can be concluded that the trend of increasing reported incidents compared to previous years continued in 2022. In 2021, a total of 672 incidents were reported to CIRT, while in 2022, CIRT recorded 684 reports.

Figure 7 Statistics of Reported Cyber Incidents 2012–2022

Year	*Attack on Websites and IS*	*Internet Scams*	*Misuse of Profiles on Social Networks*	*Inappropriate Content on the Internet*	*Malware*	*Other (Harassment, Blackmail …)*	*In Total*
2011	1	–	–	–	–	–	1
2012	3	2	–	1		–	6
2013	5	3	10	–	1	3	22
2014	5	6	20	5		6	42
2015	6	17	37	19	17	36	132
2016	18	20	36	14	50	25	163
2017	91	18	34	9	368	12	532
2018	13	68	50	6	363	37	537
2019	19	70	79	11	387	38	604
2020	25	84	90	15	383	44	641
2021	21	75	86	9	430	51	672
2022	30	81	77	6	459	31	684

266. The CIRT was located within the MPA until November 2020. However, because of amendments to the LCI, since November, it has been transferred to the Directorate for the Protection of Classified Information (DPCI). According to assessments, this organizational change has had a negative impact on the functionality of CIRT due to insufficient spatial, technical, and personnel capacities, as well as the implementation of planned activities to enhance capacities for the prevention and suppression of all types of cyber-attacks in Montenegro. In relation to this, the national Cyber Security Strategy includes the establishment of a new overarching body—the Cyber Security Agency (CSA), within which CIRT.ME would operate. The Strategy states that this approach, through mechanisms for controlling the application of basic principles and risk management, would strengthen collective cyber security and cyber defense at the national level:

Operational Goal 2	*An Effective Mechanism for Responding to Cyber Incidents*		
Performance indicator	The initial value	The target value until 2024	The target value until 2026

Operational Goal 2	*An Effective Mechanism for Responding to Cyber Incidents*		
Percentage of successfully resolved cyber incidents reported to CIRT, i.e., the Cyber Security Agency (%)	80	85	90
Number of officers to support military operations in the field of cyber security	12	16	20

267. In order to improve information security measures, as well as monitor the work and propose activities to CIRT in establishing a system for protection against computer and security incidents on the Internet, the Government of Montenegro, based on the LIS, has adopted a Decision on the establishment of the Council for Information Security (hereinafter referred to as the Council). The Council consists of representatives of the state administration body responsible for internal affairs, the state administration body responsible for defense affairs, the state administration body responsible for judicial affairs, the administration body responsible for information society affairs, the administration body responsible for foreign affairs, the administration body responsible for classified information, and the NSA, and if necessary, representatives of other bodies and institutions. The tasks of the Council are defined in its founding document, which include:

- Informing the Government of Montenegro about all-important issues related to information and cyber security.
- Initiating and proposing measures to improve information and cyber security in the public and private sectors.
- Monitoring the implementation of the Cyber Security Strategy of Montenegro 2018–2021 and action plans for its implementation.
- Monitoring and coordinating activities in the field of information and cyber security.
- Proposing measures to align the legislative and administrative framework in order to improve information and cyber security in Montenegro.
- Working on improving cooperation in the field of information and cyber security among state bodies, state administration bodies, local self-government units, legal entities performing public authorizations, and other legal and natural persons who have access to or handle data in accordance with the law regulating information security and coordinating their activities.
- Working on enhancing cooperation with the private sector in the field of information and cyber security.
- Working on enhancing international cooperation in the field of information and cyber security.
- Informing the National Security Council in the event of threats and major cyber incidents.
- Submitting an annual report on its work to the Government of Montenegro.

268. The functioning of the Council so far has highlighted the need to amend the Decision on its establishment in a way that formally allows for the possibility of inviting representatives from the private sector, academic community, and civil society to Council meetings, as needed, to discuss specific issues and foster collaboration.

269. Additionally, it is necessary to revise the section regarding the tasks of the Council to acknowledge that the Council monitors the implementation of the new Strategy for the period 2022–2026 and the action plans for its implementation.

270. Please note that any changes to the Decision would require a formal process and approval by the relevant authorities in accordance with the applicable laws and regulations.

271. This Directorate is responsible for the education and implementation of activities within its jurisdiction. It also engages in close collaboration with international partners to exchange information and enhance its capacities in the areas of certification of classified information systems, TEMPEST protection, handling cryptographic materials, and the improvement and further implementation of an information system for the exchange of domestic classified information.

272. The NSA, as defined by the Law on the NSA ("Official Gazette of the Republic of Montenegro," No. 28, May 5, 2005, "Official Gazette of Montenegro," No. 20, April 15, 2011), is primarily focused on protecting national interests and security. It is recognized as one of the key institutions in the field of cybersecurity in Montenegro. The responsibilities of the Agency include the collection and processing of data related to:

(1) activities aimed against the independence, sovereignty, territorial integrity, security, and constitutional order of Montenegro;
(2) matters of significance to defense interests and the fulfillment of strategic security goals and interests (intelligence and counterintelligence activities in the field of defense);
(3) activities related to terrorism;
(4) activities related to organized crime;
(5) the most serious forms of criminal offenses against humanity and other goods protected by international law;
(6) activities of intelligence services of other states that are of importance to national security;
(7) potential threats to Montenegro's economic interests;
(8) threats to international security;
(9) other possible threats to national security.

273. Government authorities and legal entities exercising public authority are obliged, by official duty, to inform the Agency about any data relevant to national security that they come across in the performance of their duties. Additionally, they are required to grant the Agency access to data in the registers and databases they maintain. This obligation also applies to other legal entities based in Montenegro, as well as to legal entities not based in Montenegro but whose equipment for data processing is located in Montenegro. Requests from the Agency for access to data from registers and databases or for their submission are considered classified information, and their confidentiality is determined in accordance with the law governing classified information.

274. Article 3(1) of the LCI defines classified information as "any information whose disclosure to an unauthorized person has or might have harmful consequences for the security and defense, foreign affairs, and monetary and economic policies of Montenegro."[194] In Article 4, it is defined that "information shall not be determined as classified in order to conceal crime, endanger the environment, limit competition, exceed or abuse authority, or commit any other illegal act, behavior, or administrative error."[195]

275. The Government of Montenegro prescribes methods for labeling the level of confidentiality of data. The criterion for the security classification of information is the nature of the classified information and its significance to the security and defense, foreign affairs, and financial and economic policies of Montenegro.

(1) The label "top secret" is assigned to data whose disclosure would threaten or cause irreversible economic consequences for the security and interests of Montenegro.
(2) The label "secret" is assigned to data whose disclosure could have serious economic consequences for the security and interests of Montenegro.
(3) The label "confidential" is assigned to data whose disclosure could have serious consequences for the security and interests of Montenegro.
(4) The label "restricted" is determined for data whose disclosure would have ethical consequences for the performance of the body's functions.[196]

276. The classified information labeled "top secret," "secret," and "confidential" can only be accessed by a person who has been granted permission to access secret data based on a security check. If there are no additional provisions defining declassification, the classified status will end after the term of:

(1) Thirty years for information marked as "top secret."
(2) Fifteen years for information marked as "secret."
(3) Five years for information marked as "confidential."
(4) Two years for information marked as "restricted."[197]

277. Article 9 of the Law on the NSA grants the Agency the authority to secretly collect information through the following methods:

(1) Cooperation with Montenegrin citizens and foreigners.

194. Article 3 of the Law on Classified Information of Montenegro.
195. Article 4 of the Law on Classified Information of Montenegro.
196. Article 12 of the Law on Classified Information of Montenegro.
197. Article 18 of the Law on Classified Information of Montenegro.

(2) Surveillance and observation, using technical means for documentation.
(3) Purchasing documents and items.
(4) Monitoring electronic communications and postal shipments.
(5) Surveillance of the interiors of premises, closed spaces, and objects using technical means.

278. In the implementation of these methods, the Agency may use an official document or a designation to conceal its identity, as well as the identity of the person with whom confidential cooperation has been established. The competent authority issues the document or designation at the request of the Director of the Agency and keeps a separate record of them. Upon the cessation of the reasons for which the use of the document or designation was approved, the issuing authority cancels them and delivers them to the Agency for safekeeping.

279. After joining NATO, the Ministry of Defense and the Armed Forces (MDAF) of Montenegro has made significant efforts to enhance information security, particularly in building cyber defense capabilities in line with national and NATO strategic goals. In this context, organizational structures within the MDAF have been modified, clearly recognizing the need to strengthen cyber capacities in the defense domain. Additionally, substantial resources have been invested in the implementation of technological solutions and upgrading the expertise of personnel, resulting in improved mechanisms for cyber threat prevention and response to cyber incidents.

280. At the end of 2019, the Cyber Security Strategy of the Armed Forces of Montenegro for 2019–2022 was adopted, focusing on achieving specific objectives related to the protection of information and communication systems of the MDAF, as well as defining the framework for cyber development in the field of military operations. The MDAF continues to enhance existing and develop new cyber capabilities to ensure cyber defense capacities in accordance with national and NATO strategic goals.

281. According to the Regulation on the Organization and Operation of State Administration, the MPA is responsible for various administrative tasks, including: proposing and implementing established policies in the field of establishing and developing the information society; preparing draft laws and other regulations in the field of the information society; providing expert assistance in the application of ICT in state administration bodies; establishing frameworks for managing information systems of state administration bodies and government agencies in accordance with international standards; establishing technological and security IT infrastructure in state administration bodies and government agencies; as well as determining technical and other rules for the use of ICT in state administration bodies and government agencies.

282. As the authority responsible for information and communication infrastructure and information security in state administration, in the upcoming period, to further protect the IT infrastructure, the procedures for opening new accounts (email addresses) and granting access to state information systems will be updated to include mandatory training on safe Internet usage and ICT for every new state employee and official. Additionally, in cooperation with the Personnel Administration, specific education programs will be developed for employees in PA at the state and local levels, as well as for officials.

283. Within the Police Directorate of the Ministry of Internal Affairs of Montenegro, the High-Tech Crime Unit was established in 2015 as part of the Organized Crime and Corruption Control Department (OCCCD). In line with its prescribed jurisdiction, the High-Tech Crime Unit takes measures and actions in the execution of orders issued by competent courts using standardized digital forensic tools and devices that have been validated by relevant scientific institutions specializing in digital evidence.

284. In order to enhance data protection within the Forensic Center, is currently being implemented the project LIMS (a Laboratory Information Management System) 32, which will represent the Intranet network, that is a fourth (private) network within the Forensic Center. By implementing this Intranet network, specifically the LIMS system, all data will be transferred to new hardware and software solutions that will be completely physically isolated and protected within the institution. This will enable seamless data transfer within the Forensic Center and enhance the physical protection of data against any potential cyber-attacks from external sources via the Internet.

285. However, investments in new hardware and software solutions to improve the work processes of the Forensic Center are currently insufficient, and it will be necessary to allocate the necessary funds in the upcoming period to enhance the security of computer systems from within. In addition to investing in new hardware and software solutions, it is crucial to ensure that the Forensic Center has sufficient human capacity to carry out digital forensics and effectively investigate cybercriminal activities in Montenegro.

Chapter 2. General Obligations (For EU: Transposition of the NIS Directive)

286. By signing the Stabilization and Association Agreement, Montenegro has officially undertaken the obligation to harmonize its national legislation with the EU acquis communautaire, along with commitments to establish political dialogue, improve economic relations, develop a free trade zone, ensure regional cooperation, and promote cooperation in various other areas. As a member of the UN, OSCE, and Council of Europe, Montenegro has fulfilled a significant portion of its international obligations in the previous period, including: (a) Signing and ratifying a significant number of international conventions; (b) Undertaking numerous strategic activities to align its national legislation with contemporary and international solutions addressing cyber security; (c) Making substantial transformative and operational efforts at the national level in combating cyber-attacks. Furthermore, Montenegro has become a member of the European Centre of Excellence for Countering Hybrid Threats, joined the NATO Cooperative Cyber Defense Centre of Excellence (CCDCE) in Tallinn, Estonia, and participated in numerous joint international exercises, training, meetings, forums, and conferences.

287. By enacting the LIS in 2010 ("Official Gazette of CG," Nos. 14/2010 and 40/2016), the field of information security at the national level was systematically regulated for the first time in accordance with projected needs, both in terms of its own security and the development of the information society, as well as in line with the requirements of international integration processes.

288. The law applies to state bodies, bodies of state administration, bodies of local self-government units, legal entities with public authorizations, and other legal and natural persons who access or handle data. The application of the law is limited to data whose information security is ensured in accordance with regulations governing data confidentiality.

289. Article 2 of the law defines "information security" as the state of confidentiality, integrity, and availability of data, while "data" is defined as information, a message, or a document created, sent, received, recorded, stored, or displayed by electronic, optical, or similar means, including Internet transmission and electronic mail. Under this law, data confidentiality means that the data is only accessible to authorized persons who have the right to access or handle such data. Data integrity entails preserving the existence, accuracy, and completeness of the data, as well as protecting processes or programs that prevent unauthorized alteration of the data. Data availability means that authorized users can access the data whenever they need to.

290. The law specifies that information security measures represent general rules aimed at providing basic protection of data at the physical, technical, and organizational levels. The government determines information security measures in accordance with the type of data, the risks to its security, and the type of protection. At the national level, the implementation of information security measures follows the standards prescribed by the Regulation on Information Security Standards ("Official Gazette of Montenegro," No. 019/13 dated April 19, 2013):

(1) MEST ISO/IEC 27001:2009.
(2) MEST ISO/IEC 27002:2009.

291. The envisaged measures ensure:

(1) physical protection, which includes protecting the facility, premises, and devices where data is located;
(2) data protection, which encompasses prevention and mitigation of harm from data loss, disclosure, or unauthorized modification (rules for handling data; content and manner of keeping records of data accesses; data security monitoring);
(3) protection of the information system.

292. After a major cyber-attack on the Government's information infrastructure that occurred on August 20, 2022,[198] the drafting of a new LIS was initiated in order to strengthen information security in Montenegro. The MPA identified the following key reasons for the adoption of the new law:

(1) The absence of general criteria for identifying key and important entities on which the performance of activities of public interest depends.
(2) Cybersecurity management.
(3) Lack of reporting on cyber threats and incidents.
(4) Incident resolution and response to cyber threats and incidents with significant impact.
(5) Handling and response in the event of a cyber-crisis.
(6) Absence of competent bodies responsible for cybersecurity and supervisory tasks with defined competencies.
(7) Lack of reporting obligations at the entity level.
(8) Lack of clearly defined measures regarding cybersecurity risks.

---

198. The cyber-attack primarily targeted the government's IT infrastructure and information and communication network of institutions, which were subjected to continuous cyber-attacks of high intensity and complexity. The cyber-attack disrupted the smooth operation and functioning of public administration, requiring a transition from electronic to traditional ways of conducting business. A significant number of information systems were compromised, affecting the continuity of service delivery and causing substantial damage that required a multi-phase recovery process. During the analysis, it was determined that a total of 17 information systems in 10 institutions were encrypted, and the cyber-attack directly impacted 150 computers. An expert team from the United States provided support in overcoming the situation and planning and establishing mechanisms for enhanced cyber protection in the event of future highly sophisticated cyber-attacks. Support from experts from the National Agency for the Security of Information Systems (ANSSI) of the Republic of France aided the ministry in restoring certain information systems. Experiences regarding ongoing cyber-attacks were exchanged with partners from the United Kingdom, and joint projects for enhancing information security in Montenegro were planned. (Information on the activities taken to mitigate the consequences of cyber-attacks on the government's IT infrastructure and information and communication network of institutions can be found at www.gov.me).

(9) Absence of expert oversight.
(10) Absence of penal provisions.

293. The key amendments to the LIS Security relate to the identification and procedure for recognizing key and important entities, obligations of competent sectoral authorities, and the establishment of new authorities with public powers. In this regard, it is stipulated that key entities should be identified in the following sectors: energy (subsectors: electricity; centralized heating and cooling; oil; gas; hydrogen), transportation (subsectors: air; rail; water and road transport), banking, financial market infrastructure, healthcare, drinking water, wastewater, digital infrastructure, ICT service management, PA, and space. The same provision prescribes that important entities should be recognized in the sectors of postal and courier services, waste management, production, manufacturing and distribution of chemicals, production, processing, and distribution of food, production of other important goods (subsectors: production of medical products and in vitro diagnostic medical devices; production of computers, electronic and optical products; production of electrical equipment; production of machinery and devices; production of motor vehicles, trailers, and semitrailers; production of other transport equipment), and digital service providers. The new Draft Law imposes an obligation on key and important entities to implement the international standard ISO/IEC 27001 for information security management.

294. It is also stipulated that the competent sectoral authority maintains a Register of key and important entities in the sector for which it is responsible. Sectoral criteria are determined, taking into account the characteristics of those sectors, the type and significance of services provided by that sector or subsector, as well as threshold criteria based on the assessment of the impact of cyber threats and incidents on service delivery, particularly considering losses, economic consequences, impact on national security, impact on the public, and other factors. Key and important entities are required to provide the competent sectoral authority with information on any changes in data at least once a year, based on which the competent sectoral authority is obliged to update the Sector Register.

295. Based on the submitted data and the assessment of compliance with general and sectoral criteria, the competent sectoral authority prepares a proposal list for determining key and important entities and submits it to the state administration body responsible for the development of the information society and e-government. In addition, it is stipulated that the Ministry maintains the National Register of key and important entities and the competent sectoral authority is required to provide the Ministry with data from the Sector's Register and regularly inform the Ministry about any changes in the data from the Sector's Register.

296. Article 23 of this law defines the scope of work of the Cybersecurity Agency as the central body for the field of information security with legal personality and the status of a state agency accountable to the Government. The competencies of the Agency are as follows:

(1) Prepare the professional basis for the development of strategic documents and action plans, as well as laws and bylaws within the scope of the Agency's work.
(2) Monitor and analyze comparative legal regulations and practices of EU and NATO allies and propose the implementation of best practices.
(3) Issue instructions and procedures for testing and assessing the security of network and information systems.
(4) Provide proposals and recommendations for improving information security measures.
(5) Provide early warnings, announcements, and information about risks and incidents.
(6) Implement protection against cyber threats and incidents on the network and information systems of key and important entities, excluding state administration bodies.
(7) Take action on reported incidents of key and important entities, excluding state administration bodies.
(8) Carry out operational coordination during the resolution of a cyber-crisis in cooperation with the Ministry; collaborate with the Ministry or the Government's CIRT to strengthen information security, exchange information on incidents, and their resolution methods.
(9) Monitor the state of incidents in the field of information security.
(10) Continuously conduct risk and incident analysis.
(11) Maintain a Register of reported incidents.

297. The CSA is obliged to report to the Government at least once a year on the state of incidents in cooperation with the Ministry. It conducts education for authorities, relevant sectoral bodies, and key and important entities through consultations and training to strengthen information security. It collaborates with private and civil sectors, national and international organizations, and key and important entities. It participates in the development and implementation of international projects. It carries out professional supervision over the work of key and important entities in accordance with the law. It conducts professional supervision over the implementation of information security measures by key and important entities. It conducts professional supervision over the implementation of information security measures prescribed by the international standard ISO/IEC 27001 for information security management at key entities. It performs other tasks in accordance with the law. The funds for the operation of the CSA are provided in the Budget of Montenegro, and the approved funds for the functioning and operation of the Agency cannot be less than 0.2% of the current budget of Montenegro.

298. Article 35 establishes the competencies of the Ministry in the field of information security, which include:

(1) Developing strategic documents, action plans, and regulations in the field of information security. Collaborating with private and civil sectors, national and international organizations, as well as key and important entities.

(2) Acting as the unique national contact point for information security and cooperating with the unique national contact points of other countries.
(3) Collaborating with the Agency to strengthen information security and exchanging information about incidents and their resolution.
(4) Developing the National Plan for Cyber Threats, Incidents, and Cyber Crisis Response, which determines the management of cyber threats, incidents, and cyber crises in collaboration with the Agency.
(5) Implementing protection against cyber threats and incidents on the network and information systems of government authorities. Handling reported incidents of government authorities and coordinating the incident resolution process.
(6) Maintaining a registry of reported incidents and performing other tasks in accordance with the law.

299. The draft of the new LIS Security prescribes the obligation of key and important entities to conduct an impact assessment of all cyber threats and incidents in order to identify incidents that have a significant impact on the continuity of service provision.

300. An incident, within the scope of this Law, is defined as any event that jeopardizes the confidentiality, integrity, and availability of stored, transmitted, or processed data or the services offered by network and information systems or that allows access to them.

301. The Law makes a distinction between "cyber threat" and "serious cyber threat." A "cyber threat" is defined as any possible circumstance, event, or action that could damage, disrupt, or otherwise negatively affect data and network and information systems, users of those systems, and other authorities and individuals. A "serious cyber threat" refers to a cyber threat that, based on its technical characteristics, can be assumed to have a significant impact on the network and information systems of a subject or user of the subject's services, resulting in significant material or immaterial damage. In addition to government authorities, key and important entities are obligated to provide the Agency with a monthly report on all cyber threats and incidents that they determine do not have an impact on the continuity of service provision. Key and important entities that are government authorities are also required to provide a monthly report to the Government's CIRT on all cyber threats and incidents that they determine do not have an impact on the continuity of service provision.

302. Furthermore, key and important entities are obligated to inform the Agency about all serious cyber threats that could lead to an incident with a significant impact on the continuity of service provision, as well as incidents that have a significant impact on the continuity of the services they provide. They are also required to inform the Agency about all measures they are taking or planning to take in response to a cyber threat or incident. Similarly, key and important entities that are government authorities must inform the Government's CIRT about all serious cyber threats and incidents. The participation of the Agency or the Government's CIRT, upon receiving notification of all serious cyber threats that could lead to an incident with a significant impact on the continuity of service provision, is precisely defined based on whether the incident is of low, medium, or high severity.

303. In addition, the procedure for declaring a cyber-crisis by the Government has been defined, along with the roles of the Ministry and the Agency in the event of such a declaration. A "cyber crisis" is defined as an event or situation that threatens national security, health and lives of a large number of citizens, significantly disrupts the environment, or causes significant economic damage, and requires the involvement of multiple authorities and the application of appropriate measures.

304. Although Montenegro is not a member of the EU, and therefore not obligated to implement the National Intelligence Service (NIS) Directive, the draft of the new LIS includes provisions for alignment with Directive (EU) 2022/2555 of the European Parliament and the Council of December 14, 2022, on measures for a high common level of cybersecurity across the Union, amending Regulation (EU) Nos. 910/2014 and Directive (EU) 2018/1972, and repealing Directive (EU) 2016/1148 (NIS 2 Directive).

305. In addition to the three previously adopted Cyber Security Strategies for the periods 2013–2017, 2018–2021, and 2022–2026, the strategic framework for cyber security in Montenegro also includes the National Security Strategy and the Defense Strategy of Montenegro.

306. Although significant progress has been made in establishing a strategic framework for cybersecurity in Montenegro, there is still room for further work and improvement in this field. Threats to the availability and integrity of information and communication infrastructure, privacy, and confidentiality of personal data have influenced the perception of the importance of cybersecurity and the security of cyberspace and CI. These factors have prompted an analysis of the changed environment in which the existing strategic and organizational framework for cybersecurity in Montenegro operates. The final report on the implementation of the previous Cybersecurity Strategy 2018–2021 demonstrated that the most significant progress has been made in the domains of education, regional, and international cooperation. Positive trends have been observed in the areas of capacity building for cyber defense, public-private partnerships, data protection, and strengthening inter-institutional cooperation. Planning new operational goals and performance indicators remain a prerequisite for continuous progress in these areas. However, the protection of critical information infrastructure and centralization of cyber expertise and resources have not shown satisfactory progress compared to the initial values in 2018. The main reasons for the inadequate fulfillment of strategic goals have been identified as financial factors and insufficient awareness of the importance of investing in cybersecurity at the highest levels of management.

307. The current Cybersecurity Strategy of Montenegro for the period 2022–2026 is an interdepartmental document aimed at enhancing overall capacities (legislative, operational, human, financial, and technical) to effectively respond to challenges and threats originating from cyberspace within and outside Montenegro. The strategy establishes strategic objectives and operational goals for their achievement. In line with the principles of coherence and transparency, the strategy has been prepared in alignment with the priorities and goals of Montenegro's overarching strategic documents addressing national security, defense, and digitalization. It is also in line with the Government Work Program for 2021. During the development of the strategy, the criteria for strategic planning defined in the Regulation on the Method and Procedure of Developing, Aligning, and Monitoring the Implementation of Strategic Documents were respected, as well as the guidelines from the Policy Development, Preparation, and Monitoring Methodology for Strategic Documents. This approach ensures efficient and sustainable management of cybersecurity in Montenegro.

308. The National Security Strategy of Montenegro[12] recognizes the continuous improvement of cyber defense, security, and safety systems as strategic national interests. The realization of Montenegro's strategic interests contributes to the protection of vital interests, social development, and overall prosperity. Other important interests of Montenegro, which promote the protection of vital and strategic interests and strengthen society's resilience to security challenges, risks, and threats, include reducing the crime rate with a focus on high-tech and other forms of organized crime, as well as protecting CI through fostering collaboration among state institutions, the civil sector, and the private sector to enhance civil preparedness in responding to security challenges, risks, and threats. The strategy also recognizes cyber and hybrid threats as security threats.

309. The Defense Strategy of Montenegro[13] provides long-term regulation and guidance for the development of normative, doctrinal, and organizational solutions within the defense system. It also outlines the engagement and vision for the development of defense resources in response to contemporary security challenges, risks, and threats. The strategy defines strategic goal 1: Protection of sovereignty, territorial integrity, and independence of Montenegro, and operational goal 3: Enhancement of the cyber defense, security, and safety system.

310. Within the framework of this strategy, efforts are directed toward strengthening Montenegro's defense capabilities in the cyber domain. This includes the development and implementation of measures to protect against cyber threats and ensure the security and safety of critical information systems and infrastructure. By enhancing the cyber defense system, Montenegro aims to safeguard its sovereignty, territorial integrity, and independence in the face of emerging security risks and threats in the cyber realm.

Chapter 3. Sector-Specific Obligations (E.g., Financial Sector, Health Sector, Etc.)

311. The LIS of Montenegro stipulates that critical information infrastructure consists of information systems of authorities whose disruption or destruction would endanger the lives, health, safety of citizens and the functioning of the state, and whose operations are essential for the performance of activities of public interest.

312. In order to establish a legislative framework for the protection of CI, Montenegro has enacted the Law on the Determination and Protection of Critical Infrastructure, which entered into force on January 3, 2020. The Law on the Determination and Protection of Critical Infrastructure further defines CI as systems, networks, facilities, or their parts located on the territory of Montenegro, the disruption of their functioning or interruption of supply of goods or services through these systems, networks, facilities, or their parts could have serious consequences for national security, human health and life, property, the environment, citizen safety, economic stability, or the performance of activities of public interest.

313. In accordance with the law, the protection of CI is defined as "a set of activities and measures aimed at preventing disruptions in the functioning, damage, or destruction of critical infrastructure in the event of a threat, ensuring the functioning and resilience of critical infrastructure in the event of disruptions or damage, and preventing the occurrence of consequences resulting from disruptions in the functioning, damage, or destruction of critical infrastructure."

314. For the sectors of CI in which the determination of CI is carried out, the following sectors are recognized: energy, transportation, water supply, healthcare, finance, electronic communications, ICT, environmental protection, functioning of state authorities, as well as other areas of public interest. Based on sectoral criteria established by the government, following prior risk assessments conducted by relevant ministries responsible for these sectors, and inter-sectoral criteria defined by the respective Law, CI operators assess which systems, networks, facilities, or their parts they use or manage represent CI in a particular CI sector. They provide this information to the ministry responsible for that sector. Based on this information, the respective ministries determine whether the criteria are met and submit proposals for the determination of CI for those sectors to the Ministry of the Interior, which consolidates the proposals from all ministries and submits them to the government for the final determination of CI.

315. Inter-sectoral criteria for determining CI are established based on a risk analysis that applies to all sectors of CI. A system, network, facility, or its part can be designated as CI if it meets at least one of the following criteria prescribed by Article 8:

- Potential number of casualties or injuries due to serious disruptions or cessation of CI operations.

- Economic consequences, potential economic losses and/or deterioration of product or service quality, as well as potential environmental consequences due to serious disruptions or cessation of CI operations.
- Impact on national security.
- Impact on the public, including potential consequences of disruptions or cessation of CI operations on public trust and regular life activities.

316. The protection of CI is carried out through the application of physical and technical security measures in accordance with the provisions of the Law on the Protection of Persons and Property. The protection of Critical Information Infrastructure (CII) and the protection of CI used by the state administration authorities responsible for defense, police affairs, the Armed Forces of Montenegro, and the NSA (ANB) will be carried out in accordance with a special law. They are exempt from the obligation to develop a security plan and appoint a coordinator.

317. KI operators are obliged to develop a security plan for the protection of CI and obtain the approval of the Ministry of Internal Affairs, which forms a Commission for this purpose.

318. The security plan must include:

(1) Description of systems, networks, facilities, or their parts that constitute CI.
(2) Risk analysis.
(3) Activities and measures aimed at preventing disruptions, damages, or destruction of CI in the event of a threat, ensuring the functioning of CI in case of disruptions or damages, and preventing the consequences of disruptions, damages, or destruction of CI. These include:
   - Permanent security measures (technical, organizational, communication measures, early warning measures, and awareness strengthening) that are continuously implemented.
   - Security measures taken based on the level of risk and threats to the functioning of CI.

319. In addition, KI operators are required to provide the competent ministry with information on the status or changes in the systems, networks, facilities, or the parts they use or manage at least once a year. They are also obliged to appoint a designated person for the protection of CI, known as a "coordinator," who:

(1) monitors regulations and international agreements related to the protection of CI;
(2) monitors the implementation and review of the security plan or protection plan as specified in Article 15 of this law;
(3) facilitates communication between the operator of CI and the ministry responsible for the specific sector regarding the protection of CI;
(4) prepares and conducts training for employees of CI operators on the protection of CI and keeps records of their training;

(5) provides advice to employees of CI operators regarding the protection of CI; and
(6) performs other tasks in accordance with this law.

320. The law stipulates the following requirements that a coordinator must meet:

(1) resides or has approved residence in Montenegro;
(2) holds a minimum of a level VIII educational qualification;
(3) possesses general health capability;
(4) has not been finally convicted of a criminal offense prosecuted ex officio, nor is a criminal proceeding pending against them for such a criminal offense;
(5) has professional qualifications for the protection of CI;
(6) has passed the professional exam for the protection of CI.

321. KI operators, coordinators, and other entities are obligated to use sensitive information solely for the purpose of protecting CI as prescribed by law. In the performance of their duties and when participating in data exchange related to CI, they are required to handle classified information pertaining to CI in accordance with the law governing data confidentiality.

322. The obligation to comply with data protection regulations regarding personal data related to CI is also prescribed. The protection of personal data in Montenegro is ensured through the application of the Constitution, ratified international agreements, and national legislation, primarily the provisions of the Law on Personal Data Protection (LPDP)[199] and the LFAI.[200] The Agency for Personal Data Protection and Free Access to Information plays an adequate supervisory role in the field of personal data protection. Montenegro has not harmonized its legislation with the General Data Protection Regulation (GDPR) 2016/679, and therefore, it cannot be considered to provide a level of personal data protection and privacy rights equivalent to those enjoyed by citizens of the EU.

323. The Ministry responsible for the sector of CI is required to keep records of the following:

(1) Professional examination for the protection of CI, which includes the following information:
   - ordinal number;
   - name, surname, unique identification number, gender, date, place and country of birth, and residence of the individual who passed the professional examination;
   - date of taking the professional examination;
   - examination result;

199. The Law on the Protection of Personal Data ("Official Gazette of Montenegro," Nos. 079/08 from Dec. 23, 2008, 070/09 from Oct. 21, 2009, 044/12 from Aug. 9, 2012, 022/17 from Apr. 3, 2017).
200. The Law on Free Access to Information ("Official Gazette of Montenegro," No. 030/17 from May 9, 2017).

   - certificate number of the passed professional examination and date of issuance.
(2) Approvals for security plans, which include the following information:
   - ordinal number;
   - name, headquarters, and address of the operator of CI who prepared the security plan;
   - number and date of granting approval for the security plan;
   - number of the approved security plan.
(3) Coordinators, which includes the following information:
   - ordinal number;
   - name and surname of the coordinator;
   - name, headquarters, and address of the operator of CI who appointed the coordinator;
   - date of appointment of the coordinator.

324. Operator KI is required to keep records of the following:

(1) CI, which includes the following information:
   - ordinal number;
   - number and names of systems, networks, objects, or their parts that constitute CI;
   - locations where the CI is situated;
   - information indicating that the operator of CI is not obligated to prepare a security plan in accordance with Article 14 of this law.
(2) Security Plans or Protection Plans from Article 15 of this law, which includes the following information:
   - ordinal number;
   - date of submission of the security plan to the Ministry for approval and date of receiving the approval;
   - number of the security plan or protection plan from Article 15 of this law;
   - date of the conducted revision of the security plan or protection plan from Article 15 of this law.
(3) Coordinator, which includes the following information:
   - ordinal number;
   - name, surname, unique identification number, date, place, country of birth, and residence of the coordinator;
   - date of appointment of the coordinator.

325. In the event of disruptions, damages, or destruction of CI, the coordination and management are undertaken by a coordination team established in accordance with the Law on Protection and Rescue.[201] The coordination team may include leaders and representatives of other government bodies responsible for specific sectors of CI, as well as experts in the field of CI protection.

---

201. The Law on Protection and Rescue ("Official Gazette of Montenegro," Nos. 13/2007, 5/2008, 86/2009—second law, 32/2011, 54/2016, 146/2021, and 3/2023).

326. The draft of the new LIS introduces the obligation to report cyber threats and incidents to establish a National Register of Key and Important Entities. This will allow monitoring of the state of cybersecurity by tracking the number of reported cyber threats, the extent to which they have escalated into incidents, the number of reported incidents, and their severity. In the future, it will be necessary to amend the regulations to define domain registration systems and DNS systems as critical systems, as indicated by the EU NIS Directive. Additionally, the recognition of the sector of domain registration service providers and domain management systems should be ensured, along with the necessary harmonization of existing laws in the field of protection of CI and information security.

Chapter 4. Liability and Remedies

327. The LCI prescribes misdemeanor liability for the legal entity in Montenegro if:

(1) fails to set the information as classified and mark its classification level at the moment of establishing or receiving it or at the moment of beginning with preparations for establishing such information;
(2) during the designation of classification levels, it does not assess the harmful effects on the security of the state and its interests;
(3) fails to determine the classification level of the information resulting by connecting two or more pieces of information or does not separate a piece of information and determine its level of classification;
(4) fails to inform all the bodies and organizations using such information on its reclassification;
(5) does not appropriately mark classified information;
(6) accesses classified information without a security clearance;
(7) carries out the vetting procedure without the written consent of the person cleared;
(8) fails to provide insight into the requested information on the request of the Agency;
(9) delivers classified information to another user without the previous consent of the authorized person who determined the classification level of such information;
(10) fails to inform the Directorate about changes in information from a previously submitted security questionnaire with evidence;
(11) fails to immediately inform the authorized person of noticed irregularities pertaining to the protection of classified information;
(12) fails to immediately take measures in order to eliminate noticed irregularities or measures for the prevention or reduction of possible harmful effects of the disclosure of classified information;
(13) fails to ensure constant monitoring of classified information given to the user and keep updated records;
(14) fails to take measures and activities providing administrative, physical, and industrial protection of classified information;
(15) fails to immediately inform the authorized person who determined the classification level of the loss or unauthorized disclosure of classified information within the body or organization where such information is lost or within the body or organization to whom such information is delivered;
(16) fails to immediately take all necessary steps to identify the circumstances that caused the loss of classified information or its disclosure to an unauthorized person, remove any harmful effects, and prevent further losses and unauthorized disclosure of such information;
(17) fails to keep records on classified information, issued and revoked security clearances and security permissions;

(18) fails to ensure regular internal control over the implementation of protection measures regulated by the law.'[202]

328. A possibility of monetary fines is provided, ranging from EUR 1,100 to EUR 16,000 for legal entities as well as a responsible person within a body or legal entity—between two and twenty times the minimum salary in Montenegro.

329. The LPDP stipulates a sanction between EUR 500 and EUR 20,000 for any legal entity that:

(1) engages in the processing of personal data without the data subject's prior consent;
(2) fails to delete personal information from a personal data storage system within thirty days of a request;
(3) processes special categories of personal data contrary to the provisions of the law;
(4) processes personal information related to criminal and misdemeanor proceedings illegally;
(5) processes personal data for commercial purposes and through other forms of advertising without the data subject's consent;
(6) entrusts the tasks of personal data processing falling within his area of responsibility to a processor of personal data who is not registered for carrying out the processing of personal data or who does not meet the requirements for implementation of technical, personnel, and organizational measures for the protection of personal data;
(7) does not maintain records of personal data that have been shared with beneficiaries, the purpose for which they were shared, or the legal basis for the use of personal data;
(8) fails to delete personal information whose processing violates the law;
(9) does not provide technical, personnel, and organizational safeguards to protect personal data against loss, destruction, unauthorized access, modification, disclosure, and abuse;
(10) establishes a personal data filing system before seeking consent from the agency or before the expiration of the thirty-day time limit from the date the request was submitted;
(11) does not maintain or update personal information file systems;
(12) supervises in a manner that displays recordings of apartment building interiors unrelated to entrances to residential and commercial areas or records apartment entrances;
(13) fails to inform the personnel operating in areas under video surveillance in writing about the effectiveness of video surveillance;
(14) conducts video surveillance in commercial or official locations outside of the working post;

202. Article 82 of the Law on Classified Information of Montenegro.

(15) fails to notify employees in writing of the implementation of video surveillance prior to the commencement of video surveillance;
(16) utilizes a video surveillance system to capture apartment entrances;
(17) fails to provide a visible public notification of video surveillance;
(18) includes insufficient information in the public notification of video surveillance;
(19) fails to prevent unauthorized access to the video surveillance system used to conduct video surveillance;
(20) fails to notify the data subject within fifteen days of the receipt of the request;
(21) fails to amend, delete, or restrict the use of personal data within fifteen days of the date the request was submitted;
(22) fails to notify the data subject, or his legal representative or attorney, as well as the recipient of the personal data, of the rectification, erasure, or restriction of the use of the personal data;
(23) as a recipient or processor fails to comply with an Agency order or prohibition.

330. In addition, a responsible person of a legal entity, state, or other authority shall be fined between EUR 150 and EUR 2,000.[203]

331. The current Law on the Protection of Critical Infrastructure prescribes misdemeanor liability for the operator of CI who:

(1) fails to annually submit to the competent ministry responsible for a specific sector of CI information on the status or changes in the systems, networks, facilities, or their parts used or managed by them, designated as CI;
(2) fails to develop a security plan and obtain approval from the Ministry;
(3) does not comply with instructions for amending and updating the Security Plan within ninety days;
(4) fails to revise the security plan once every five years or in the event of changes in the functioning of the systems, networks, facilities, or their parts used or managed, designated as CI;
(5) fails to appoint a coordinator from among the employees within six months from the date of adopting the act designating the systems, networks, facilities, or the parts they use or manage as CI;
(6) employs an individual who does not meet the qualifications for a coordinator according to this law;
(7) fails to provide the Ministry with data on the coordinator within fifteen days from the date of their appointment and fails to notify them of any changes to that information within five days from the date of such changes;
(8) does not exclusively use sensitive information for the purpose of protecting CI as prescribed by this law.

---

203. Article 74 of the Law on the Protection of Personal Data of Montenegro.

332. A possibility of monetary fines is provided, ranging from EUR 2,000 to EUR 15,000 for legal entities, as well as responsible individuals in competent state bodies, state administration bodies, local self-government bodies, and local government bodies, in the amount of EUR 200 to EUR 1,000.

333. Unlike the current LIS, which does not prescribe penalty provisions, the Draft Law introduces administrative liability for legal and natural persons registered as key subjects in the National Register if they:

(1) fail to provide data to the competent sectoral authority;
(2) do not submit an annual notification of changes to the data specified in Article 16(1) of this law;
(3) do not implement information security measures;
(4) fail to designate an employee responsible for monitoring the implementation of information security measures;
(5) do not apply the international standard ISO/IEC 27001 for information security management;
(6) do not provide the Agency with a monthly report on all cyber threats and incidents determined to have no impact on the continuity of service provision;
(7) do not notify the Agency of all serious cyber threats that could lead to an incident significantly affecting the continuity of service provision, as well as incidents significantly affecting the continuity of the services they provide, and fail to provide information on the measures they are taking or planning to take in response to cyber threats or incidents;
(8) fail to inform recipients of their services about all serious cyber threats and incidents that could have a negative impact on the provision of their services, as well as the measures that recipients should take in response to cyber threats and incidents;
(9) do not submit an initial notification of an incident significantly affecting the continuity of service provision within twenty-four hours of discovering the incident;
(10) do not submit the first report during the incident significantly affecting the continuity of service provision, at the latest within seventy-two hours of submitting the initial notification of the incident, which must contain a detailed description of the incident and its actual and potential consequences, in accordance with the criteria specified in Article 38 of this law;
(11) do not submit additional reports on the incident significantly affecting the continuity of service provision during the incident, if they become aware of new data or circumstances relevant to the incident;
(12) do not submit a final report on the incident significantly affecting the continuity of service provision, at the latest within thirty days from the day of resolving the incident, which must include information about the incident, an analysis of its causes, measures taken to respond to the incident, and measures taken to prevent its recurrence;

(13) deny the inspector or supervisor access to premises, computer equipment, and devices and fail to promptly provide the necessary information and documentation related to the subject of supervision.

334. The prescribed monetary fines range from EUR 500 to EUR 20,000 for legal entities and from EUR 30 to EUR 1,500 for individuals. In case of repeated offenses, a ban on conducting activities may also be imposed for a period of three to six months.

335. Article 56 of the same Law also provides for administrative liability for a legal entity that:

(1) fails to implement information security measures;
(2) fails to submit a monthly report to the Agency on all cyber threats and incidents that have no impact on the continuity of service provision;
(3) fails to notify the Agency of all serious cyber threats and incidents;
(4) denies the inspector or supervisor access to premises, computer equipment, and devices and fails to promptly provide the necessary information and documentation related to the subject of supervision.

336. The prescribed monetary fines range from EUR 500 to EUR 5,000 for legal entities and from EUR 30 to EUR 1,500 for individuals. In case of repeated offenses, a ban on conducting activities may also be imposed for a period of three to six months.

337. By introducing professional and inspection supervision, the Draft LIS establishes the responsibility of key and important entities for the implementation of prescribed information security measures and the issuance of prescribed acts on cyber security risks.

Part VI. Cybercrime

Chapter 1. Application of International and Regional Agreements (E.g., Status of the Council of Europe Cybercrime Convention, Law Enforcement Cooperation Agreements, Etc.)

338. Article 9 of the Constitution of Montenegro establishes the legal status of international treaties and generally accepted rules of international law within the national legal framework. According to this article, once international treaties are confirmed and published, they become an integral part of Montenegro's legal system. In cases where international treaties and domestic legislation regulate the same matter differently, the international treaty takes precedence and is directly applied.

339. This provision ensures that Montenegro complies with its international obligations and recognizes the primacy of international law over domestic legislation. By incorporating international treaties into its legal framework, Montenegro aims to align its laws and practices with international standards and promote cooperation with other nations in various fields, including law enforcement, human rights, trade, and diplomacy.

340. In 2005, Montenegro signed the Convention on Cybercrime of the Council of Europe (Budapest Convention) with the objective of harmonizing national legislation and strengthening cooperation in cybercrime criminal investigations. By signing the Budapest Convention, Montenegro demonstrated its commitment to addressing the challenges posed by cybercrime and aligning its legislation with international standards. Through the implementation of the Budapest Convention, Montenegro seeks to improve its capabilities in preventing, investigating, and prosecuting cybercrimes, as well as to promote international cooperation in this field. Following that, with the enactment of the Law on Confirmation of the Convention on Computer Crime four years later, the convention was ratified alongside the Additional Protocol on Racism and Xenophobia and the Convention on the Protection of Children from Sexual Exploitation and Sexual Abuse (CETS 201). After ratification, Montenegro harmonized its criminal law with the provisions of these Conventions in an effort to strengthen the institutional and regulatory framework for responding to assaults on information systems and combating child pornography on the Internet.

341. The harmonization of national legislation with the Cybercrime Convention referred to changes in substantive criminal law, i.e., introducing four new categories of criminal offenses into the Montenegrin legal system:

(1) criminal offenses against the confidentiality, integrity, and availability of computer data and systems (unauthorized access, unauthorized interception, interference with data, interference with systems, and misuse of devices);
(2) computer-related crimes (computer-related forgery and computer-related fraud);
(3) criminal offenses in relation to the content (criminal offenses related to child pornography); and
(4) criminal acts related to the violation of copyright and similar rights.

342. In May 2020, Montenegro signed the second additional protocol to the Convention on Computer Crime on enhanced cooperation and the discovery of electronic evidence. The protocol has been signed in order to reinforce cybercrime-fighting cooperation between Montenegro and other countries and international organizations (Europol, Interpol, Eurojust, etc.). The protocol has not yet been ratified, and it is expected that its ratification will significantly strengthen the capacities of national judicial and other competent authorities in collecting evidence in electronic form for the purpose of specific criminal investigations and proceedings through additional tools for more effective international assistance in criminal matters.

Chapter 2. Specific Computer Crimes (Unlawful Access, Identity Theft, Online Fraud, Online Sabotage, Forgery)

343. The XVIII title of the Montenegrin Criminal Code prescribes six criminal offenses against computer security, as follows:

(1) damage to Computer Data and Programs;
(2) computer System Interference;
(3) creating and Inserting Computer Viruses;
(4) computer Fraud;
(5) unauthorized Access to a Computer System;
(6) abuse of Devices and Programs.

344. Article 142 of the Criminal Code defines a "computer program" as a "movable article or object," under which term is also considered any generated or collected energy for the production of light, heat, or movement, as well as a telephone impulse. Other key terms related to computer-related offenses are defined in the same article as follows:

(a) a computer system is defined as any device or group of interconnected or dependent devices that one or more rely on to perform automatic data processing;
(b) computer data is referred to as a collection of facts, data, or concepts in a format that is suitable for processing in a computer system, involving the programs that enable a computer system to perform or carry out its functions;
(c) a computer program is considered to be a structured set of computer data that allows a computer system to perform its functions;
(d) a computer virus is a computer program that affects or modifies the functions of a computer system and jeopardizes or inappropriately utilizes computer data;
(e) computer traffic data is described as all computer data created by computer systems that participate in a chain of communication between two computer systems involving themselves.[204]

345. The damage to computer data and programs is governed by Article 349 of the Criminal Code of Montenegro, which states, "whoever unauthorizedly deletes, alters, damages, conceals, or otherwise renders unusable computer data or programs shall be punished by a fine or imprisonment for a term not exceeding one year." If the damage exceeds EUR 3,000, the perpetrator is eligible for a prison sentence between three months and three years, and if the damage exceeds EUR 30,000, the perpetrator is eligible for a prison sentence between three months and five years.[205]

346. Article 350 regulates interference with computer systems. It states: "whoever intentionally enters, destroys, deletes, alters, damages, conceals, or otherwise

204. Article 142 of the Criminal Code of Montenegro.
205. Article 349 of the Criminal Code of Montenegro.

renders inoperable computer data or computer systems shall be punished with a fine or imprisonment for a term not to exceed three years." If such an offense is committed with regard to data and programs that are significant to state authorities, public services, institutions, business organizations, or other entities, the perpetrator shall be punished with a prison term of one to eight years, and the devices used to commit the offense shall be confiscated if they are the perpetrator's property.[206]

347. Article 351 of the Criminal Code of Montenegro regulates the creation and insertion of computer viruses: "Whoever creates a computer virus with the intent to insert it into another person's computer system shall be punished with a fine or a term of imprisonment not exceeding one year." If the perpetrator inserted a computer virus into another person's computer system and caused damage, he may be punished with a monetary penalty or a maximum two-year prison sentence.[207]

348. Article 352 of the Montenegrin Criminal Code regulates computer fraud. It states, "Whoever enters, alters, deletes, fails to enter correct data, otherwise conceals or falsely represents computer data, or otherwise interferes in any manner with the functioning of a computer system, thereby influencing the result of electronic processing, transfer of data, and functioning of a computer system with the intention of obtaining unlawful material benefit for himself or for another and thereby causing property damage to another, shall be punished by a fine." If this offense results in a material benefit exceeding EUR 3,000, the perpetrator shall be punished with a prison term of two to ten years, and if the offense results in damage exceeding EUR 30,000, the perpetrator shall be punished with a prison term of two to twelve years.[208]

349. Article 353 of the Criminal Code of Montenegro covers unauthorized access to a computer system: "Whoever unlawfully accesses a computer system in its entirety or in part shall be punished with a fine or a term of imprisonment not to exceed one year." If this offense is committed by violating measures for computer system protection or by unauthorized access to a computer system of relevance to state authorities, local government authorities, or institutions provided with public authority, the offender is subject to a fine or a prison sentence of up to three years. Whoever illegally intercepts non-public computer data, regardless of the method of transmission, during its transmission to, from, or within a computer system, including electromagnetic emissions, will be subject to this penalty.[209]

350. Article 354 of the Criminal Code of Montenegro regulates the misuse of devices and programs, which includes selling, procuring for use, importing, distributing, and making otherwise accessible:

---

206. Article 350 of the Criminal Code of Montenegro.
207. Article 351 of the Criminal Code of Montenegro.
208. Article 352 of the Criminal Code of Montenegro.
209. Article 353 of the Criminal Code of Montenegro.

(1) devices and computer programs designed or adapted primarily for the commission of any of the criminal offenses against computer security; and
(2) computer codes or similar data through which one can access a computer system in its entirety or parts thereof with the intent to use it for the commission of any of the criminal offenses against computer security shall be punished by a prison sentence for a term from three months to three years.[210]

210. Article 354 of the Criminal Code of Montenegro.

Chapter 3. Traditional Crimes in a Digital Context (Offenses Against Decency, Hate Speech, Defamation, Etc.)

351. According to the recommendations of the Council of Europe, Montenegro decriminalized defamation and slander in 2011. However, the Criminal Code's Article 197 regulates the dissemination of information regarding private and family life. It states, "whoever states or disseminates information about the personal or family life of a person that could undermine his honor or reputation shall be punished with a fine ranging from three thousand to ten thousand euros, and if the offense was committed using the media or similar means or at a public gathering, the perpetrator shall be punished with a fine ranging from five thousand to fourteen thousand euros."[211]

352. In addition, Article 370 of the Criminal Code defines inciting national, ethnic, or religious enmity as a criminal offense. It states that anyone who publicly incites violence or hostility against a group or a member of a group based on race, skin color, religion, origin, state, or national affiliation will be sentenced to between six months and five years in prison.[212]

211. Article 197 of the Criminal Code of Montenegro.
212. Article 370 of the Criminal Code of Montenegro.

Chapter 4. Criminal Procedural Aspects (Incl. Data Retention, Interception of Electronic Communications, Network Search, Seizure of Data, Duties of Intermediaries)

353. All criminal procedural aspects in Montenegro are governed by the Criminal Procedure Code (Official Gazette of Montenegro, Nos. 57/09, 49/10, 47/14, 2/15, 35/15, 58/15, 28/18, and 116/20), which contains several definitions that are important for the investigation and processing the computer crimes.

354. The provisions of the Criminal Procedure Code of Montenegro resolve issues related to the conduct of criminal investigations, primarily the interception and control of communications on the Internet, cross-border access to information, and modalities for conducting verification of Internet users in emergency situations.

355. The criminal procedure legislation in Montenegro is mainly harmonized with the EU's certain procedural provisions in the field of cybercrime.

356. Amendments to the Criminal Code would focus on penal policy regarding criminal offenses related to the spread and transmission of false news and disinformation, while amendments to the Criminal Procedure Act would improve and facilitate investigative misconduct.

357. The VII Chapter of the Criminal Procedure Code of Montenegro, named "Evidentiary Actions," prescribes reasons for searches of dwellings, other premises, movable articles, and persons in Article 75. The search of movable articles within the meaning of paragraph 1 of this article shall include the "search of computers and similar devices for automatic data processing to which the computer is connected. At the request of the court, the person using a computer shall enable access to the computer and removable storage used for storing information relative to the object of the search (discs, USB flash discs, USB hard discs, diskettes, tapes, and alike), as well as give necessary information on the use of the computer."[213]

358. An individual can refuse to do so only on the grounds of Article 111 (Denial of Answer to Specific Questions), which refers to witnesses' right not to answer particular questions if it is likely that they would thus expose themselves or persons that are exempted from the duty to testify to serious disgrace or criminal prosecution.[214] The persons that shall be exempted from the duty to testify are referred to in Article 109 as follows:

(1) the accused persons' spouses and their extramarital partners;
(2) accused persons' direct blood relatives, collateral blood relatives up to the third degree, as well as their relatives by marriage up to the second degree;

213. Article 75 of the Criminal Procedure Code of Montenegro.
214. Article 111 of the Criminal Procedure Code of Montenegro

(3) accused persons' adopted children or adoptive parents, or accused persons' foster parents and foster children.[215]

359. Article 82 of the Criminal Procedure Code of Montenegro governs the seizure of certain objects on the basis of a search warrant. It states that "if certain objects are seized during the search of computers and similar devices for automatic data processing, they shall be immediately returned to their users if they are not needed for further procedure." The same Article prescribes that personal information obtained during such an investigation may be used only for the purposes of conducting a criminal procedure and shall be erased as soon as that purpose ceases.[216]

360. Article 156 states that photographs or audio or audiovisual recordings of evidentiary activities conducted in accordance with the law may be used as evidence in criminal proceedings if they have been authenticated if the possibility of photo installation, video installation, or other forms of falsification of photographs and recordings has been excluded, and if they have been made with the implicit or express consent of the suspects or accused persons when their image or voice is on the photograph or the recording.[217]

215. Article 109 of the Criminal Procedure Code of Montenegro.
216. Article 82 of the Criminal Procedure Code of Montenegro.
217. Article 156 of the Criminal Procedure Code of Montenegro.

Selected Bibliography

Boardman, John. The Prehistory of the Balkans and the Middle East and the Aegean World. Cambridge University Press, 1982.

European Commission. "Eurydice, Montenegro: Historical Development." Accessed June 28, 2019. https://web.archive.org/web/20190628190256/https://eacea.ec.europa.eu/national-policies/eurydice/crna-gora/historical-development_me.

Jelena Danilović. "Foreword to Valtazar Bogišić, General Property Code for Principality of Montenegro." Belgrade—Official Gazette, Podgorica—Unirex, 1998.

Jokić, Lj. "State Legal History of Montenegro." Podgorica, 2002.

Kamusella, Tomasz. The Politics of Language and Nationalism in Modern Central Europe. Palgrave Macmillan, 2009.

European Union External Action. "The European Union and Montenegro." Accessed [insert date]. https://www.eeas.europa.eu/montenegro/european-union-and-montenegro_en?s=225.

European Bank for Reconstruction and Development. "Investor Perceptions and the Broadband Sector: South Eastern Europe Region & Montenegro." Brussels: Cullen International, 2020.

Monstat, Statistical Office of Montenegro. Statistical Yearbook 2022.

Law on Electronic Communications. Official Gazette of Montenegro, No. 040/13 from Aug. 13, 2013, 056/13 from Dec. 6, 2013, 002/17 from Jan. 10, 2017, 049/19 from Aug. 23, 2019.

Law on the Use of Physical Infrastructure for the Installation of Electronic High-Speed Communication Networks. Official Gazette of Montenegro, No. 001/22 from Jan. 10, 2022.

Agency for Electronic Communications and Postal Service of Montenegro. "Work Report for the 2022 Year." Podgorica, 2023.

Law on Digital Broadcasting. Official Gazette of Montenegro, No. 34/11.

Institute for Research Development in the Field of Occupational Safety. "Study on the Strategy of Introducing 5G Mobile Communication Networks in Montenegro." Podgorica, 2021.

The Strategy for the Development of 5G Mobile Communication Networks in Montenegro 2023–2027.

Agency for Electronic Communications and Postal Services. "Overview of the Electronic Communications Market in Montenegro." 2023.

Selected Bibliography

Agency for Electronic Communications and Postal Services. "Register of Electronic Communication Service Providers in Montenegro." Accessed March 28, 2023. https://ekip.me/table/electronic-communications/ek-operators-register.

Vujica Lazovic, Tamara Djurickovic. "Economic Analysis of the e-Government Development in Montenegro." Montenegrin Journal of Economics, No. 12, Vol. VI, 104.

The Digital Transformation Strategy of Montenegro 2022–2026.

The Smart Specialization Strategy of Montenegro (S3) 2019–2024.

The Cybersecurity Strategy of Montenegro 2022–2026.

The Accession Program of Montenegro to the European Union for the period 2022–2023. https://www.eu.me/wpfd_file/program-pristupanja-crne-gore-evropskoj-uniji-2022-2023/.

The Agency for Electronic Communications and Postal Services. https://ekip.me/.

Criminal Code of Montenegro. Official Gazette of Montenegro, No. 57/2009 and 3/2020.

Criminal Procedure Code of Montenegro Official Gazette of Montenegro, No. 57/2009, and 116/2020.

Index

The numbers here refer to paragraph numbers.

Index

www.ingramcontent.com/pod-product-compliance
Lightning Source LLC
Chambersburg PA
CBHW071344230926
51846CB00002B/448
9789403539775